The

DIALECTICAL BEHAVIOR THERAPY DIARY

SECOND EDITION

Monitoring
Your Emotional
Regulation
Day by Day

JEFFREY C. WOOD, PsyD
MATTHEW McKAY, PhD

New Harbinger Publications, Inc.

Publisher's Note

NEW HARBINGER PUBLICATIONS is a registered trademark of New Harbinger Publications, Inc.

Distributed in Canada by Raincoast Books

Copyright © 2021 by Matthew McKay and Jeffrey Wood
New Harbinger Publications, Inc.
5674 Shattuck Avenue
Oakland, CA 94609
www.newharbinger.com

Cover design by Amy Shoup

Acquired by Jess O'Brien

Edited by Madison Davis

All Rights Reserved

Library of Congress Cataloging-in-Publication Data

Names: Wood, Jeffrey C., author. | McKay, Matthew, author.
Title: Dialectical behavior therapy diary : monitoring your emotional regulation day by day / Jeffrey C. Wood, Matthew McKay.
Description: 2nd edition. | Oakland, CA : New Harbinger Publications, [2021] | Revision of: The dialectical behavior therapy diary / Matthew McKay, Jeffrey C. Wood. c2011. | Includes bibliographical references.
Identifiers: LCCN 2020047208 (print) | LCCN 2020047209 (ebook) | ISBN 9781684037735 (trade paperback) | ISBN 9781684037742 (pdf) | ISBN 9781684037759 (epub)
Subjects: LCSH: Dialectical behavior therapy.
Classification: LCC RC489.B4 M425 2021 (print) | LCC RC489.B4 (ebook) | DDC 616.89/142--dc23
LC record available at https://lccn.loc.gov/2020047208
LC ebook record available at https://lccn.loc.gov/2020047209

Printed in the United States of America

24   23   22

10   9   8   7   6   5   4   3   2

Contents

Preface to the Second Edition

Since the introduction of dialectical behavior therapy (DBT) in the early 1990s, by Marsha Linehan, PhD (Linehan 1993a), DBT has successfully been used around the world to help people struggling with overwhelming emotions and borderline personality disorder. However, in the last twenty-seven years DBT has also evolved and demonstrated effectiveness for treating other mental health problems, such as depression, post-traumatic stress disorder, shame, anger, substance abuse, and more. In response, many clinicians and researchers have further added to the treatment to expand its usefulness. The result has led to Linehan publishing a new edition of her *DBT Skills Training Manual* (2015), as well as we, the authors of this book, publishing the revised second edition of *The Dialectical Behavior Therapy Skills Workbook* (McKay, Wood, and Brantley 2019). The improved treatment now includes skills such as values clarification, problem solving, exposure-based cognitive rehearsal, compassion meditations, physiological coping skills, and more—many of which you'll find in this book too.

In order to help you practice DBT in the most effective way, New Harbinger Publications also offers *The Dialectical Behavior Therapy Skills Card Deck: 52 Practices to Balance Your Emotions Every Day*. Many of the skills in the card deck are also included in this *DBT Diary*, and are marked with a symbol (*) so you can use them in conjunction with the cards.

We hope you find this *DBT Diary* a useful tool in your treatment. We are continually working to make DBT more effective and understandable, as the treatment itself continues to grow and include more skills.

—Matthew McKay, PhD

—Jeffrey C. Wood, PsyD

Dialectical Behavior Therapy

What Is DBT?

Dialectical behavior therapy (DBT) was originally created by Dr. Marsha Linehan (1993a) to help people who were struggling with borderline personality disorder. It was designed to teach people practical skills to improve their lives, and research showed that it was very successful. Now DBT is also being used to help people who are struggling with a wide variety of other problems, including depression, bipolar disorder, and anxiety. The common factor in all of these problems is overwhelming emotions.

Overwhelming Emotions

People who struggle with overwhelming emotions often feel vulnerable. At any point, the smallest trigger can lead to a tidal wave of emotions that leaves them feeling confused, angry, alone, hopeless, and in pain. Because of this, people who struggle with overwhelming emotions often try desperately to maintain control of their feelings, their relationships, the actions of others, and their environments. But no matter how hard they try, something always seems to go wrong and once again they get overwhelmed by their feelings. Some people with this problem have been struggling with it since childhood. Others are also dealing with the devastating impact of early physical, emotional, or sexual abuse. In addition, many of them struggle with problems like dysfunctional relationships, interference with their schoolwork or job, health problems, dangerous or self-harming behaviors, and an inability to focus or concentrate. The combined result of all these issues can be truly painful, both emotionally and physically.

The Four DBT Skills Groups

Luckily, DBT has successfully taught thousands of people how to cope with issues related to overwhelming emotions. In general, DBT teaches four groups of practical skills that will help you in many areas of your life:

1. *Distress tolerance* skills will help you distract from painful situations when you can't cope with them, and then relax and soothe yourself.

2. *Mindfulness* skills will help you stay focused on what's happening in the present moment, concentrate, and make healthier choices as a result.

3. *Emotion regulation* skills will help you identify and name your feelings, and then learn how to tolerate them without getting overwhelmed.

4. *Interpersonal effectiveness* skills will give you the tools to improve your relationships, ask for what you want in an effective way, say no, and establish appropriate boundaries, in a respectful, healthy way.

The Purpose of This Book

This book, *The Dialectical Behavior Therapy Diary*, will teach you many of the skills from the four groups. It was written as a companion to *The Dialectical Behavior Therapy Skills Workbook* (McKay, Wood, & Brantley 2019), where you will find in-depth explanations of each of the four skills groups, as well as additional exercises in each category.

This diary is designed to enhance the progress that you've already made in individual DBT treatment, in DBT group treatment, or on your own using *The Dialectical Behavior Therapy Skills Workbook*. (If you aren't already familiar with DBT skills, you might want to consult *The Dialectical Behavior Therapy Skills Workbook* or a DBT therapist for assistance.)

In general, this *DBT Diary* has three purposes:

- To remind you of the core DBT skills in each of the four groups

- To record your successes each time you use one of the skills

- To help you observe and record the overall improvements in your life due to using these skills on a daily basis

Many people in DBT treatment mistakenly think that they're using the skills more often than they really are, or they don't remember the small successes they have using their skills. Either way, they don't make improvements as quickly as they could. The goal of this book is to help you become more active in your treatment and find out for yourself what kind of impact the skills are having on your daily life.

How to Use the Diary

After the five chapters of this book, which review the core skills in each of the DBT skills groups, you'll find enough blank diary pages for fifty-two weeks—an entire year of recording your progress using DBT. In order to optimize your use of this diary, you'll need to do three things:

- Learn the skills and practice them as often as possible.

- Be sure to record the number of times you use each skill every day. For the fastest improvements, record each skill as soon as you use it. But at the very least, record your skills at set times throughout the day, maybe at lunch and dinner, or at the end of each day before you go to sleep. Don't wait until the next day or the end of the week since you might forget.

- And most importantly, note in the diary how you feel at the end of each day. It's very important to see if there's a connection between using the coping skills and improving your mood. This is the evidence you'll need to determine if the treatment is working. Hopefully you'll notice, over time, that the more coping skills you use every day, the better you feel.

When you record your mood, use a number from 0 to 10 and do your best to be consistent. For example, maybe 0 means you feel the worst you've ever felt in your whole life and you need to go to the hospital because you feel like you might die. A rating of a 5 might mean that you feel average, neither very good nor very bad. And a 10 might indicate that you feel so fantastic and fulfilled that it's one of the best days of your life. Whatever criteria you choose, continue to use it every day.

We wish you luck in your treatment. If you commit to using your DBT skills every day, you'll surely see positive results. But remember, if at any point you have too hard a time implementing the skills, please consult a qualified DBT therapist.

CHAPTER 1

Distress Tolerance

Sometimes it's difficult or impossible to avoid a situation that causes you emotional or physical pain. As a result, you might feel overwhelmed and not know what to do. In situations like these, distress tolerance skills can help you endure and cope with the situation until you're able to come up with a plan to deal with the situation in a healthy, effective way. There are fourteen important distress tolerance skills that you should learn and use every day:

- Stop self-destructive actions

- Use the "REST" strategy

- Use radical acceptance

- Distract yourself from pain

- Engage in pleasurable activities

- Soothe yourself

- Practice relaxation

- Commit to valued action

- Rehearse values-based behavior

- Engage with your higher power

- Use coping thoughts

- Determine feelings-threat balance before coping (FTB-Cope)

- Use coping strategies

- Use physiological coping skills

Stop Self-Destructive Actions

Some people who struggle with overwhelming emotions also engage in self-destructive actions, like cutting, burning, or scratching themselves. If this is something you do, the most important first step in your treatment is to stop these behaviors or engage in some safer type of behavior instead. While it's true that some of these actions might release your body's own painkillers and make you feel good temporarily, it's also true that they can lead to serious infection, injury, and possibly death.

Here are some safer actions you can use to distract yourself from self-destructive emotions and thoughts:

- Hold an ice cube in one hand and squeeze it.

- Write on yourself with a red felt-tip marker instead of cutting.

- Draw faces of people you hate on balloons and pop them.

- Throw foam balls, rolled-up socks, or pillows against the wall as hard as you can.

- Make a voodoo doll out of rolled-up socks or foam, then stick pins in it.

In your diary, note how many times each day you're able to stop yourself from engaging in self-destructive actions.

Use the REST Strategy*

Changing any habit is difficult, especially when you've been behaving a certain way for a long time and seem to react automatically in troubling situations. Changing behaviors is also very difficult when you get really upset and can't even think about what else to do in a problematic situation. The REST strategy can help facilitate behavior change even when you're in a challenging spot (*see card #11 in *The DBT Card Deck*). REST is an acronym for:

Relax

Evaluate

Set an intention

Take action

REST is a helpful reminder to yourself to slow down, think about what's happening, and use healthier coping strategies. Do your best to use the REST strategy rather than act impulsively and possibly do harm to yourself or others (physically or emotionally).

Relax The first step to take in any difficult emotional situation is to simply stop! Don't do what you usually do. Don't act impulsively. Stop, breathe, and pause before you react automatically—and emotionally—to the troubling situation. You might even say "Relax" out loud, or "REST" to remind yourself. Pausing and relaxing before you act will give you a few seconds to breathe and think about what to do next.

Evaluate The next step is to figure out what's happening in the current situation. You don't need to conduct a full analysis of the problem, but you do need to get a general sense of what's bothering you. Now is the time to ask yourself questions like: "What am I thinking, feeling, and doing *right now?*" "What is happening with the other people involved in this situation?" and, "What's causing the problem that I'm having?"

Set an Intention The third step is to create a simple plan of action. Again, this is a simple plan, not a complicated one. If there is a bigger problem to solve, you're probably not going to solve it at this moment while you're emotionally upset. But maybe ask yourself, "What can I do about it right now? What action can I take to solve this problem?" This is the time to use one of the DBT coping skills that you've already learned. Hopefully, you've practiced several of the skills in each of the categories and can remember enough of the steps to pick one and use it.

Take Action The final step of the REST acronym is to take action—to put your plan into motion. If you set your intention to use an interpersonal skill like assertive communication, now is the time to use it. If you picked a mindfulness skill like mindful breathing, or a distress tolerance skill like self-soothing, go ahead and do the actions associated with these skills now.

Again, the REST strategy is like an emergency response plan. Rather than panicking during a troubling, emotional situation—and possibly acting impulsively and destructively—do your best to relax, evaluate, set an intention, and take skillful action. With enough rehearsal and practice using REST, you will become able to perform these steps in just a few seconds and make this process a new habit, replacing the old, ineffective behavior.

Using REST one time might not solve the entire, bigger problem that's causing the situation. But you can use REST more than once in the same situation, giving yourself a path to choosing to act in a way that's healthier and more helpful to you. You can practice using the REST strategy in imaginary problematic situations, or even try to predict when you might need to use it in real life so that you can anticipate what coping strategies might be effective.

In your diary, note how many times each day you use the REST strategy.

Use Radical Acceptance*

Radical acceptance (* see card #10 in *The DBT Card Deck*) is the ability to acknowledge whatever is happening to you right now without fighting it, judging the event, or criticizing yourself and others (Linehan 1993b). For example, imagine that you're stuck in a long line at the grocery store. You might start to get angry and judge other people for being so slow or criticize yourself for being "so stupid" for shopping at this time, or you might start to argue with the manager to open a new checkout line. However, all of these thoughts and behaviors will only make your situation more frustrating and painful. In addition, if you think, "This situation shouldn't be happening," you're missing the point that it *is* happening, so you must deal with it as best you can.

In comparison, radical acceptance helps you acknowledge that your situation is occurring because of a long chain of past events that you can't control or fight. Using radical acceptance might not make the long line at the grocery store move any quicker, but it will prevent you from creating additional frustration and suffering for yourself. Use some of the following coping statements to help you practice radical acceptance in challenging situations:

- "For better or worse, this is the way it has to be right now."

- "It won't help the situation to criticize myself or anyone else right now."

- "It's no use fighting the past, because I can't do anything to change it."

- "This situation is the result of past decisions I can't change anymore."

- "The present is the only moment I have any control over."

When you use radical acceptance, it also creates an opportunity for you to recognize the role you and others are playing in the current situation so that you can choose to do something more effective. For example, if the line at the grocery store is much too slow and you have other obligations, it might be better to just leave than to get angry. Here are some key questions to ask yourself:

- "What past events led up to this situation?"

- "What role did I play in creating this situation?"

- "What role did others play in creating this situation?"

- "What do I have control of in this situation?"

- "What is beyond my control in this situation?"

- "If I radically accept this situation, what choices can I make?"

Keep in mind that radical acceptance doesn't mean that you have to condone or agree with bad behavior in others or surrender to dangerous situations. For example, if you're in an abusive relationship and you need to get out, then get out.

In your diary, note how many times each day you use radical acceptance.

Distract Yourself from Pain*

Sometimes when you're feeling overwhelmed by your emotions or you're experiencing too much pain, it's impossible to cope with a difficult situation. In these circumstances, the best that you can do is distract your attention and focus on something else (*see card #2 in *The DBT Card Deck*). Then, with a little time, you'll be able to relax and cope with the situation in a healthy, effective way. Here are some ways to distract your attention:

- *Pay attention to someone else.* Volunteer to help someone, go to a shopping mall or park to observe other people, or simply think of having a peaceful, soothing conversation with someone you care about.

- *Think of something pleasant.* Remember a fun event from your past in as much detail as possible, observe the natural world around you (like the trees, animals, and sky), or daydream about your most pleasant fantasy coming true.

- *Start counting.* Count whatever you can think of, like the number of breaths you take, the number of objects you see in a room, or simply numbers in order ("One, two, three…")

- *Do some tasks or chores.* Although it might not sound fun, sometimes the most mundane tasks can take your mind off something more painful.

- *Go somewhere.* Sometimes leaving a difficult situation is better than sticking around and feeling overwhelmed, especially if you're able to create a coping plan while you're gone.

Remember, the plan is not to avoid difficult situations altogether. Rather, it is to temporarily distract yourself until you can handle the situation. In other words, "Distract, relax, and cope."

In your diary, note how many times each day you're able to distract yourself from pain.

Engage in Pleasurable Activities*

Doing something pleasurable is often the best way to distract yourself from painful emotions (*see card #1 in *The DBT Card Deck*). But it's also important to engage in these types of activities on a regular basis in order to bring some joy into your life. So be sure to schedule at least one pleasurable activity every day and mark it on your diary. Here are a few suggestions:

- Spend time with friends or family

- Exercise

- Go for a long walk or drive

- Learn a new sport, skill, or hobby

- Go shopping

- Eat something delicious

- Watch a funny movie

- Visit a local café

- Listen to some upbeat, happy music and dance

- Visit a local museum

- Do something exciting, like skiing, surfing, or kayaking

- Work on your garden, car, or home

- Cook a new recipe

In your diary, note how many times each day you engage in a pleasurable activity, and record what the activity was in the "NOTES" column.

Soothe Yourself*

If you struggle with overwhelming emotions, learning how to soothe yourself is very important because it can make both your body and your mind feel better (*see cards #3, 4, and 5 in *The DBT Card Deck*). And as a result, you'll also be able to cope with difficult situations in a more effective way. The following techniques require you to use one of your five senses: smell, sight, hearing, taste, and touch. Find the ones that work best for you:

- *Use your sense of smell.* Burn incense or pleasantly scented candles. Wear scented oils. Go someplace with a pleasant scent, like a bakery. Cook something that has a pleasing smell. Buy flowers that smell nice.

- *Use your sense of sight.* Go through magazines and cut out pictures that you like and make a collage. Find a place that's soothing to look at, like a park. Look through a book of photographs or art that you like. Look at a picture or image of someone you care about.

- *Use your sense of hearing.* Listen to soothing music, an audiobook, or a pleasant talk show on the radio. Listen to the peaceful sounds of nature, like birds or the ocean. Use a white noise machine to block out distracting sounds.

- *Use your sense of taste.* Enjoy your favorite meal. Eat something soothing, like ice cream. Drink something soothing, like hot chocolate. Eat a ripe and juicy piece of fruit. Suck on a piece of your favorite hard candy.

- *Use your sense of touch.* Hug someone you care about. Carry something soft or velvety in your pocket that is soothing. Take a long, relaxing shower or bath. Get a massage or facial. Ask someone you trust to rub your shoulders or head. Wear your most comfortable clothes.

In your diary, note how many times each day you're able to soothe yourself.

Practice Relaxation*

Relaxation techniques (*see card #8 in *The DBT Card Deck*) can help you release stress from both your muscles and your mind. As a result, you'll feel calmer and more empowered to take on difficult or painful tasks. Relaxation techniques are like other skills and require practice in order to be effective. Don't wait until you're already feeling overwhelmed to try these techniques. Practice them on a daily basis so you'll be ready when you're confronted by a stressful situation:

- *Take a time-out.* If you feel burned-out from taking care of others all the time, find a little time every day to take care of yourself and your own needs. Try scheduling a half hour or hour dedicated to relaxing, exercising, reading, or even running errands for yourself. Remember, you deserve to be treated as kindly as everyone else, and it doesn't mean you're selfish if you put yourself first sometimes. Do your best to find a balance between taking care of yourself and others so that you don't end up feeling resentful or angry.

- *Use slow breathing.* Find a comfortable place to sit or lie down for five to ten minutes. Place one hand on your stomach. Inhale slowly and smoothly through your nose and imagine your breath moving down into your belly, gently expanding it like a balloon. Then exhale smoothly through your mouth and feel your belly release, like a balloon gently contracting. Find a slow, natural rhythm for breathing. When you get distracted, return your focus to your breathing or the sensation of your hand on your stomach. Do your best to relax. If you begin to feel light-headed or experience tingling in your lips or fingertips, you're probably breathing too deeply, in which case you should stop, breathe naturally, and wait until you feel better before trying again.

- *Use progressive muscle relaxation.* The goal of this technique is to release muscle tension as you exhale. You can practice while standing, sitting, or lying down, whichever is more comfortable. First, take a breath and hold it. Next, tense one group of muscles at a time for seven seconds and notice the sensation of tightness in the muscles. Finally, exhale and quickly release the tension in that muscle group. Notice the difference between the tense feeling and the relaxed feeling after you've released the muscles. You can systematically tense and release your muscles from your toes up to the top of your head, or you can group the muscles in the following way: First, curl your toes. Second, straighten your legs and point your toes. Third, bend your arms at the elbows and tighten your fists like a body-builder posing. Fourth, tighten your stomach and chest muscles by curling forward like you're hugging a large beach ball. Fifth, straighten your arms and raise your shoulders toward your ears. And finally, tighten the muscles of your eyes, mouth, and face. If you experience any pain, stop immediately.

- *Visualize a peaceful scene.* Find a comfortable place to sit or lie down for five to ten minutes. Close your eyes and use two minutes of slow breathing to help you relax. Then visualize a real or imaginary place where you feel peaceful and safe, such as relaxing at the beach, sitting on a cloud, walking in a park, sitting in an ancient temple, or any other place you like. Use your imaginary senses to ground yourself in the scene. Visualize what your peaceful scene looks like. Imagine the sounds you would hear. Try to feel anything you might be touching with your hands or other parts of your body. Imagine any smells or scents you'd experience. And finally, imagine tasting anything you might be eating or drinking. Remember, you're in control of this scene, so you can make anything appear or disappear to make it safer and more soothing. Explore your scene as fully as possible and notice any feelings or thoughts that come to you. Use this technique when you need to relax, but don't use it if you're already dissociating, or feeling detached from reality. If you are feeling detached from reality, do your best to ground yourself in the present moment by noticing what you're seeing, feeling, hearing, smelling, and touching.

In your diary, note how many times each day you use relaxation skills.

Commit to Valued Action*

Values are principles or standards that give your life meaning and point you in the right direction, like street signs. They can also help you endure tough experiences. If you're not sure what your values are, you probably need to give this some thought and define them. Or if you're engaged in behaviors that contradict your values, you probably need to act in ways that strengthen them in your life (*see card #7 in *The DBT Card Deck*).

One way to define your values is to think of the core areas that give your life meaning. For each person these will be different, but here are some common areas:

- Self-care

- Family

- Friendships

- Romantic relationships

- Others and community

- Work

- Education

- Money

- Fun

- Religion/spirituality

- Travel

- Sports

Once you've identified which of these areas are important to you, ask yourself how important they are to you on a scale of 0 to 10, with 0 being not important and 10 being the most important. Then ask yourself how much effort you're currently putting into each area, with 0 being no effort and 10 being the most effort you can apply. The difference between each area's importance and your effort indicates how much more work you need to do to make your life feel fulfilling. For example, if your family ranks as a 10 in importance but your effort is only a 4, the difference of 6 represents how much additional effort you need to make to feel fulfilled. The larger the difference, the more effort it will take.

In order to close the gap, make a true commitment to take valued action, even if it's just a small step in the right direction. For example, maybe you can commit to setting aside one hour on Saturday afternoons to take your children to the park, or maybe you can commit to working less overtime in order to be home for dinner three nights a week. State one commitment for each valued area. Be specific about what you commit to doing, set reasonable goals that you can accomplish, and set a time for when you will start.

In your diary, note how many times each day you commit to valued action, and record what the valued area of life was in the "NOTES" column.

Rehearse Values-Based Behavior*

Putting your values into action can be difficult (*see card #12 in *The DBT Card Deck*). You're likely to encounter obstacles either from other people or from yourself. Other people might be judgmental about or resistant to you acting on your values, or your own thoughts and fears might get in the way: "I can't do this" or "I'm too nervous to act on my values." But rather than let this fear stop you, we encourage you to rehearse what you want to do, just like athletes do before a game and musicians do before a performance. Imagining yourself acting on your values-based behaviors—including overcoming the resistance and obstacles—is called *cognitive rehearsal* (Cautela 1971; McKay & West 2016). Using this strategy, you can imagine yourself acting on your values with confidence, overcoming any barriers you encounter, and picturing yourself successfully accomplishing your goals.

Here are the steps to using cognitive rehearsal in order to practice your values-based behavior:

- Imagine the situation and environment in which you want to act on your values. Where are you? Who are you with? What is the situation? Try to imagine as much of the setting as you can to make it as realistic as possible.

- As you continue to imagine the situation, identify your intentions for the situation. What are the values you are putting into action and what do you want the outcome to be?

- Now identify the actions you need to take in this situation. Do your best to imagine each step of the action and what specifically you need to do at each step.

- Next, recognize any barriers or obstacles that might occur while completing your actions—barriers created by yourself, like critical thoughts and feelings of anxiety, as well as barriers created by other people, like judgments. Do your best to imagine the situation long enough to anticipate all the major obstacles that might arise.

- Now, go back to the beginning of the scene and complete a full imaginary rehearsal of the situation. Picture yourself in the scene, acting according to your values, and successfully completing your values-based behaviors step-by-step. Notice any distressing thoughts or feelings that arise while completing your actions, but imagine yourself successfully tolerating them and overcoming any other obstacles.

- Finally, imagine other people responding well to you as you successfully complete your values-based behaviors and accomplish your goals. Imagine feeling proud of yourself for acting on your values rather than acting impulsively and doing what you normally do—like avoiding or lashing out at others.

- Then repeat the whole imaginary cognitive rehearsal process one more time. Once again, imagine yourself successfully acting on your values, overcoming obstacles, accomplishing your goals, and feeling proud of yourself for succeeding.

Now you're ready to act upon your values-based behavior in real life. Pick an opportunity as soon as possible to put your cognitive rehearsal skills into action. In your diary, note how many times each day you rehearse values-based behaviors or put them into use in your life.

Engage with Your Higher Power

To some people, a "higher power" means God, but it can have many other meanings: the power of love, the spirits of nature, or the goodness of fellow human beings. No matter what it means to you, it can often be helpful to put your faith in something bigger than yourself during times of distress. Some people connect to their higher power through prayer, meditation, reading, and song, but those aren't the only ways. Each day, find a way to connect with your higher power and experience the strength and comfort that come from doing so. Here are some more suggestions:

- Write about the beliefs that give you strength and comfort.

- Visit a church, synagogue, temple, or spiritual group that you wish to learn more about.

- Set aside quiet time to think about your higher power.

- Write a letter to your higher power.

- Read books about a faith or religion you're interested in.

- Go outside and experience nature: look up at the stars, go to the beach, visit a park, or take a vacation to a place you consider sacred.

In your diary, note how many times each day you connect with your higher power.

Use Coping Thoughts*

Your thoughts directly influence how you feel and what you do. When your thoughts are self-critical, you probably feel bad about yourself and engage in behaviors that make you feel even worse. However, thoughts can have a positive effect too, especially when you're in a distressing situation. Sometimes a few supportive words in the form of a coping thought are all the help you need to accomplish a task, feel better, or get through a tough situation (*see card #9 in *The DBT Card Deck*). Here are a few suggestions:

- "This situation won't last forever."

- "I've gotten through tough times like this in the past, and I'll get through this one too."

- "My feelings are uncomfortable right now, but eventually they'll go away."

- "This is an opportunity for me to learn how to cope with my fears."

- "I'm strong enough to handle what's happening to me right now."

- "It's okay to feel sad, anxious, or afraid sometimes."

- "So what?"

- "This sucks, but it's only temporary."

- "This too shall pass."

- "My thoughts don't control my life, I do."

In your diary, note how many times each day you use coping thoughts, and record what the thoughts were in the "NOTES" column.

Determine the Feelings-Threat Balance Before Coping (FTB-Cope)*

Strong negative emotions like anxiety and anger are often accompanied by even stronger urges to react impulsively in ways that are not healthy. For example, many people who struggle with overwhelming emotions often feel threatened in some way—by another person or a situation—and in response they defend themselves by lashing out, isolating themselves, or avoiding the problem completely. However, in many of these situations the person's reaction is far bigger than the actual threat level. For example, on a scale of 1 to 10, maybe the urge to lash out at someone is a 9, but the actual threat the person is presenting is only a 2. Or maybe the urge to avoid a problem is a 10, but the actual danger that the problem presents is only a 3.

The reason many people overestimate the threat level is due to *emotional reasoning*. This is the belief that says, "Because I feel it, it must be true." For example, "I feel angry, so someone must be trying to harm me," or, "I feel alone, so someone must have abandoned me." But many times, this isn't true. Many times, a feeling is just a feeling and not an actual threat. Sometimes emotions get triggered by a random thought or sometimes they are triggered by a situation that is only slightly similar to something that happened in the past. But clearly, responding to every negative emotional experience as if it was a significant threat can be unhealthy—or even harmful—to both you and those around you. So what's the alternative?

Instead of acting impulsively to what you perceive to be a threat, do your best to determine the feelings-threat balance of the situation (*see card #13 in *The DBT Card Deck*) and then use your DBT coping skills instead (*FTB-Cope*). Although it might sound hard to do this when you're feeling emotionally overwhelmed, with practice you can complete this process in just a few seconds. In short, FTB-Cope requires you to 1) rate the intensity of your emotion, 2) rate the intensity of the threat, and then 3) pick an appropriate response.

So first, rate the intensity of your sad, anxious, or angry emotion on a scale of 0 to 10, with 0 being no distress, 5 moderate distress, and 10 the greatest distress you can imagine.

0	1	2	3	4	5	6	7	8	9	10

Low Distress	Moderate Distress	High Distress

Second, rate the actual level of the threat using the same 0 to 10 scale, with 0 = no damage, harm, or loss; 5 = moderate; and 10 = excessive. This can sometimes be difficult to assess, so try asking yourself questions to help get an accurate answer. If you're feeling angry, ask yourself, "How much damage has the person (or situation) actually caused me?" For anxiety and fear, maybe ask yourself, "How truly harmful is this situation and what is the likelihood it will actually occur?" Or for sadness, ask, "How serious is my loss?" or "How serious are the results of my actions?"

0	1	2	3	4	5	6	7	8	9	10

Low Harm, Damage, Loss	Moderate Harm, Damage, Loss	High Harm, Damage, Loss

Now compare the level of your emotion to the level of the perceived threat. Are the numbers approximately equal, like emotional level = 9 and potential harm = 8? If so, maybe your assessment of the situation is accurate and you really do need to take immediate action. In this case: 1) use the "wise mind" coping skill to make an appropriate informed decision; 2) take action based on your values; or 3) use problem-solving to determine what to do. However, if there's a large gap between your emotion and the perceived threat, like emotional state = 9 and potential harm = 3, then do your best not to react impulsively. Instead, do your best to cope first using a distress tolerance skill, such as the REST strategy, self-soothing, taking a time-out, using mindfulness, practicing radical acceptance, or using coping thoughts. Then, after you've been able to soothe your emotions to a level that's more appropriate to the potential harm, use one of the other three DBT coping strategies mentioned above as necessary.

In your diary, note how many times each day you use feelings-threat balance before coping.

Use Coping Strategies

It pays to be prepared for a distressing situation, especially if it's a situation that happens regularly. For example, maybe every time you visit a certain relative you get criticized, or perhaps every time you sit down to pay your bills you feel overwhelmed. In these cases, it's helpful to have several coping strategies ready.

To begin, make a list of several distressing situations you've experienced in the past few months. Next, record how you coped with them and list what the negative consequences were. For example, a young woman named Jane wrote, "I visited my mother, who began criticizing me, so I went into the bathroom and started cutting my arm, and then I started yelling at her. The negative consequences were that I got another scar and our relationship continues to get worse."

Next, review the distress tolerance skills you've learned and practiced in this chapter and identify those that have been most helpful. Then, for each distressing situation you identified on your list, record at least one coping strategy you could have used in that situation and identify what the healthier consequences might have been. For example, Jane wrote, "Next time, I can take a walk around the block, go to the bathroom and use slow breathing, say a silent prayer for strength, or use the coping thought 'This won't last forever.' Then I'd feel more relaxed and be able to deal with my mother in a healthier way."

After you've identified new coping strategies for each distressing situation on your list, group them into skills that you can use when you're with other people and skills that you can use when you're alone. For example, progressive muscle relaxation might be effective when you're alone and have time and space to stretch, but it might be awkward or embarrassing to do when you're with someone else. Similarly, taking a warm bath can be relaxing at home, but you probably can't do it when you're at work.

Finally, take an index card and record all the coping strategies you can use when you're alone on one side and all the coping strategies you can use when you're with others on the opposite side. Then keep the card with you in your purse or wallet to remind yourself what to do the next time you're in a distressing situation.

In your diary, note how many times each day you use coping strategies, and record what the strategies were in the "NOTES" column.

Use Physiological Coping Skills

Sometimes engaging your brain's natural reflexes to stimuli or your body's natural response to exercise can be the best way to cope with distressing emotions. Below are a few exercises that you can use to trigger your nervous system's relaxation response. Because some of these techniques can quickly affect your heart rate and blood pressure, you should check with a medical professional before trying them. This is especially important if you are taking medication or being treated for medical issues, such as a heart condition, breathing problems, high blood pressure, or pregnancy.

Side-to-Side Eye Movements

As simple as it sounds, moving your eyes from side to side several times—for about thirty seconds—has been shown to have both positive relaxing effects (Barrowcliff, Gray,

MacCulloch, Freeman, & MacCulloch 2003) and has been shown to reduce the power of painful memories (Barrowcliff, Gray, Freeman, & MacCulloch 2004).

Instructions: Practice this technique when you can relax and are not bothered by over-whelming emotions. Do not use this technique while you are driving or doing something else potentially dangerous. Be sure to do this exercise while seated or lying down, so you don't get dizzy. Start with your eyes open and move your eyes from left to right at a rather quick pace, approximately one back-and-forth movement per second, as if you were watch-ing a game of ping pong. (If it bothers you to have your eyes open, you can also try the technique with your eyes closed.) Do your best to move your eyes and not your head. If you feel any eye-strain or start to feel dizzy, stop.

If the technique feels comfortable, continue by recalling a mildly disturbing memory and then notice the emotional response you have to it now. Rate the emotion on a scale of 0 to 10, with 10 being the worse distress you can imagine. Now again, move your eyes from side to side at a rather quick pace for about thirty seconds. Don't try to hold on to the disturbing memory, rather, let whatever emotion or memory arises next to come natu-rally. Then stop, breathe, relax, and rerate your emotion. Do another four or five sets of thirty seconds until you notice a decrease in emotional distress. Each time, recall the original disturbing memory, but let it go after you start moving your eyes.

If this technique helped you with a mildly disturbing memory, try using it with increas-ingly distressing memories. With practice, you can use it in the moment the next time you experience a painful or heightened emotion (provided you are someplace safe to do so). Remember to rate your emotion before and after the eye movement, so you can notice a decrease in intensity. If you are somewhere without privacy, you can try using the eye movements with your eyes closed. Some people have even found this technique to be helpful when they are having trouble sleeping. Try the side-to-side eye-movement tech-nique while lying in bed; imagine that your eyes are "erasing" the thoughts or emotions that are keeping you awake. Do four or five sets, and then try going to sleep again.

Use Cold Temperatures to Relax

There are two ways that using cold temperatures can help you relax. The first tech-nique is called the *diving reflex* (Gooden 1994), because it occurs when you hold your breath and immerse your face in cold water. Doing so can be helpful because it slows your heart rate and turns on your body's natural relaxation response (Kinoshita, Nagata, Baba, Kohmoto, & Iwagaki 2006). However, rather than immersing your face in water, we rec-ommend that you try placing a very cold, wet towel (colder than 70 degrees Fahrenheit) or a semimelted ice pack wrapped in a towel on your forehead or cheeks. Never place a fully frozen ice pack directly on your skin, as this can cause injury. Also, be careful not to obstruct your breathing, but rather try holding your breath for several seconds (as long as is comfortable) while pressing the cold towel on your forehead or cheeks. This will be a very close approximation of the diving reflex.

Another technique to try is the *cold pressor technique*. In one psychological study that involved participants who were diagnosed with borderline personality disorder placing their hands in buckets of ice water, some participants noticed a reduction in anger, confusion, depression, and anxiety after just two to four minutes (Russ et al. 1992). You too can use the cold pressor technique, but rather than use a bucket of ice water, we recommend running your hands under very cold water from your faucet. (The water used in the experiments was 32 to 50 degrees Fahrenheit.) Or try holding onto a covered ice pack, a very cold can of soda, or even a semifrozen bottle of water for two to four minutes. This technique will likely cause you some discomfort, but if at any point it causes pain or severe discomfort, stop immediately.

As with the side-to-side eye-movement technique, try rating your emotional distress level before and after using either of these techniques, on a scale of 0 to 10, so that you can recognize any decrease in intensity.

High Intensity Interval Training (HIIT) Exercise

Physical exercise has been shown to have positive effects for people struggling with mental health issues, such as anxiety and depression (Ströhle 2009). It has even been shown to have positive effects similar to taking antidepressant or antianxiety medications (Dishman 1997). However, for many people, physical exercise is often too time consuming and not enjoyable (Trost, Owen, Bauman, Sallis, & Brown 2002). Fortunately, high intensity interval training (HIIT) is a type of physical exercise that is less time consuming, generally more enjoyable than other forms of exercise (Jung, Bourne, & Little 2014), and offers the same health benefits as doing other exercises for longer (Gibala & McGee 2008).

HIIT typically involves exercising very intensely for a short period of time—like thirty seconds to two minutes—and then exercising at a more moderate level for the same amount of time, usually going back and forth between the two "intense-moderate" pairings four to ten times. Many people perform HIIT exercises either on stationary bicycles, treadmills, elliptical machines, rowing machines, or even running outside. During the intense period of exercise the goal is to elevate your heart rate to approximately 90 percent of your maximum heart rate (Gibala, Little, MacDonald, & Hawley 2012), but if that sounds like too much to start with, pick a lower target, like 70 percent.

One way to measure your heart rate is to wear a heart-rate monitor that you can buy online or at a sporting goods store. But an easy way to estimate your heart rate on your own is to use the "talk test" (Downing 2016). It's been suggested that if you can easily talk or sing while exercising, then you're exercising at a low-intensity level. If you can talk but can only sing a few words, you're exercising at a moderate-intensity level. If you can only speak a few words and can't sing at all—because you're breathing very heavily—then you're exercising at a high-intensity level. Do your best to maintain this high level of intensity during the brief intensive period of exercise, and then slow down enough so that you can breathe and speak more easily during the moderate period of exercise.

As with any form of physical exercise, consult a medical professional before starting a routine, and before any cycle of HIIT exercise, perform a slower "warm-up" routine. Also, if you are new to HIIT exercise programs, start with shorter time intervals (like thirty seconds of high intensity followed by thirty seconds of moderate intensity), a shorter number of complete paired intervals (like three or four), or a lower maximum heart-rate target (like 70 percent) until you develop more strength and stamina and can increase your goals.

Slow Breathing

Mindful breathing has already been discussed as a distress tolerance skill, but slow breathing is so important—and helpful—that it is worth repeating here. In general, breathing at a slow pace turns on the part of your nervous system that helps you rest and relax. In many studies, breathing at a slow pace, and especially exhaling at a slow pace, have been shown to be very relaxing (McCaul, Solomon, & Holmes 1979; Lehrer & Gevirtz 2014). Breathing as slowly as six breaths per minute—one breath in and out every ten seconds—was especially relaxing to the participants in several studies (Clark & Hirschman 1990). However, for most people, breathing this slowly is challenging because the average person takes nine to twenty-four breaths per minute. So slowing your breath to six per minute should be a goal, but not a starting place.

To begin using this technique, first set a timer for one minute and count the number of breaths you normally take. Next, divide sixty seconds by that number of breaths. For example, if you counted twenty breaths, sixty divided by twenty equals three, which means you took one breath every three seconds. Now, using either a timer or a breathing app on your smartphone (there are many free breathing apps available online), slow your breathing rate by one or two seconds longer than you just counted. In this example, you might set a goal of breathing in and out every five seconds (which would be twelve breaths per minute). Most breathing apps will allow you to program the length of each breath and give you a visual aid to follow as you breathe in and out. But without a breathing app, just do your best to watch the seconds on your timer. Then over the next several weeks, progressively increase the length of your breathing exercises by one or two seconds, moving toward the goal of breathing every ten seconds or six breaths per minute.

While using this technique, remember that in addition to breathing slowly you should also do your best to make your exhalations slightly longer than your inhalations. So, for example, if you are going to breathe every five seconds, try breathing in for two seconds and exhaling for three seconds. Or, if you are going to breathe every seven seconds, try breathing in for three seconds and out for four seconds. Just do your best to make your exhalation slightly longer if you can, as this will help you relax. If at any point during this exercise you feel dizzy, light-headed, or experience tingling in your fingers or lips, stop the exercise and breathe normally. This type of experience typically indicates that you are hyperventilating and breathing too rapidly.

With practice, you can incorporate slow breathing into your daily life, especially when you are feeling overwhelmed by emotions and need a quick way to relax.

Instructions: Find a comfortable place to sit and relax. Set your timer or smartphone app for three to five minutes. Place one hand on your abdomen and allow your abdomen to expand as you breathe in, and allow it to gently deflate as you breathe out. This will help you stay focused on your breathing. If it's comfortable, inhale through your nose and exhale slowly through your mouth, as if you are blowing out candles. As you watch your timer or app, slowly breathe in through your nose, feel your abdomen expand, and silently count the length of your inhalation: "one, two" (in this example). Then slowly exhale through your mouth, allow your abdomen to deflate, and silently count the length of your exhalation: "one, two, three" (in this example). Continue this way, slowly breathing and counting the length of both your inhalations and your longer exhalations, until your timer runs out.

Use Progressive Muscle Relaxation

Progressive muscle relaxation (PMR) is a technique that involves systematically tightening and loosening your muscles to help you relax and reduce anxiety (Jacobson 1938; Wolpe 1958). To practice PMR, you gently tense and then release your muscles, and then take several seconds to notice the released, relaxed feeling of letting go of the tension. Some people also use a *cue-word* when they release their muscle tension, like "peace" or "calm," which they can then use later to help themselves relax. Many people start using PMR by actively tensing their muscles for about five seconds and then quickly releasing the tension in order to relax the muscles, but with practice, they progress to holding the tension in their muscles very lightly, and eventually progress to simply imagining their muscles releasing tension without tightening them at all. Try using all of these techniques as you practice PMR. However, never tighten any muscles to the point of feeling pain, especially as you tense muscles in your back and neck, or any place where you regularly experience pain. Also, when you release the tension in the muscles, do so quickly, so you can really notice the difference between the tight feeling and the relaxed feeling. Try to practice PMR regularly, a few times a week, especially when you are first learning this technique. Then, with regular practice, you'll be able to notice tension in your body during your daily life and quickly be able to release it. While there are various forms of PMR, below are the instructions for a shortened version of the exercise (Davis, Eshelman, & McKay 1980).

Instructions: This shortened version of PMR includes five basic poses that group muscles you can tense and release together. Before each pose, inhale and hold your breath. Then hold the tension of the pose for about five seconds before quickly exhaling and releasing the tension. Notice the relaxed feeling in your muscles. Repeat the procedure once or twice more for each pose and notice the relaxed feeling each time you release the tension. You can also say a cue word (like "relax") each time you release tension. Again, with regular practice, you might even progress to holding more subtle amounts of tension in your muscles or even just imagining yourself holding and releasing the tension.

- Inhale and hold. Clench your hands into fists, flex your biceps and forearms, and raise your arms like a bodybuilder posing for an audience. Feel the tension in your hands, arms, shoulders, and upper back. Then exhale and release the muscle tension. (Repeat)

- Inhale and hold. Attempt to place your left ear on your left shoulder and then slowly roll your chin down to your chest. Continue to slowly roll your head until your right ear nearly touches your right shoulder. Then reverse the roll and return your head to your left shoulder by moving your chin down past your chest again. Feel the tension in your neck, upper back, and jaw as your head slowly rolls. Exhale and release the muscle tension. (Repeat)

- Inhale and hold. Contract all the muscles in your face and shoulders, squeezing your face and pulling up your shoulders as if you just ate a sour lemon. Contract the muscles around your eyes, mouth, forehead, and shoulders. Then exhale and release the muscle tension. (Repeat)

- Gently arch your shoulders back and stretch your chest. Then take a full breath, expanding your chest and abdomen. Hold the breath for five seconds while noticing the tension in your chest, shoulders, back, and abdomen. Then exhale and release the muscle tension. (Repeat)

- Inhale and hold. While either lying down or sitting in a chair, straighten your legs and point your toes back toward your face. Feel the tension in your upper and lower leg. Then exhale and release the muscle tension. Now inhale and hold, and with your legs straightened point your toes away from your face. Again, feel the tension in your upper and lower leg, then exhale and release the tension. (Repeat)

In your diary, note how many times each day you use physiological coping skills.

CHAPTER 2

Mindfulness

If you struggle with a problem like overwhelming emotions, your own thoughts can sometimes be your worst enemy. For example, how many times have you had experiences like these?

- Getting caught up in criticisms about yourself or others that just made your situation more painful

- Completely missing what someone was saying to you because you were thinking about something else, and then the person got mad at you for not listening

- Not recognizing that a situation or relationship was making you upset, so you stayed in it much too long, until you were finally so frustrated that you exploded in anger

- Failing to notice that you were in a dangerous situation because you weren't paying attention to what was happening until it was too late

These types of painful experiences are caused by a lack of attention to what you're thinking, feeling, and doing.

In comparison, imagine if you could develop a skill that would help you pay better attention to what you were thinking, feeling, or doing at any given moment so that you could make healthier decisions and better choices that would improve your life. This skill does exist; it's called *mindfulness*. Mindfulness is "the ability to be aware of your thoughts, emotions, physical sensations, and actions—in the present moment—without judging or criticizing yourself or your experience" (McKay, Wood, & Brantley 2007, 89). This means that instead of getting distracted by your thoughts, worries, regrets, and criticisms, you pay attention to what's happening to you in the moment so that you can make choices about what to do next. This might sound difficult, but mindfulness is one of the most important core skills of dialectical behavior therapy (Linehan 1993a), so it deserves lots of time and practice.

In any one moment of time there might be a dozen things to be aware of: how you're sitting or standing, the sounds you're hearing, what you're thinking about, what someone else is saying, the way you're breathing, what you're doing, what someone else is doing, physical pain that you're experiencing, the texture of something you're holding, how you're feeling emotionally, and so on. And then in the next second, all of these things might change. Mindfulness means that you're aware of what's happening to you and around you ("Now I'm listening") and you're also aware of how those things are affecting you ("Now he's saying something that's making me upset").

It might sound impossible that you could be aware of all these stimuli at one time. However, with a little practice you can learn how to shift your attention so that you become more aware of each of them. For example, a moment of mindfulness might sound like this: "Now I'm aware that I'm slumping in my chair, I'd better sit up... Now I'm aware that I'm breathing in a funny way, I should relax and breathe more mindfully... I just noticed the music outside my window and the sound of trucks driving past... I'm such an idiot for what I said last night. Okay, now I'm criticizing myself and being unmindful, I need to pay attention to what I'm doing."

Remember, the goal is to do the best you can. No one is mindful all the time. In a typical day you might catch yourself being unmindful a hundred times. When you do, just gently refocus your attention on whatever you're thinking, feeling, or doing, and let go of any criticisms or judgments that might distract you.

This chapter focuses on seven important skills that will help you develop your overall mindfulness:

- Practice mindful breathing

- Use wise mind

- Practice beginner's mind

- Practice self-compassion

- Use mindful communication with others

- Do what's effective

- Complete a task mindfully

Many people are aware of these skills from other disciplines. Mindfulness, also known as meditation, has been practiced for thousands of years by many religions, including Buddhism, Hinduism, Christianity, Judaism, and Islam. However, you don't have to be religious to enjoy the benefits of mindfulness. Mindfulness is currently used in lots of successful psychological treatments for many different problems.

Practice Mindful Breathing*

Mindful breathing (*see card #19 in *The DBT Card Deck*) is the core skill of all meditation practices. It has three main purposes:

- Helping you relax as you notice the physical sensation of your breath moving in and out

- Helping you focus by counting your breaths or thinking "inhale...exhale..."

- Helping you let go of distracting thoughts by first noticing them and then returning your focus to your breathing

Mindful breathing uses the diaphragm muscle at the bottom of your rib cage. To use your diaphragm correctly, sit or lie down in a comfortable position and place one hand on your chest and one hand on your abdomen. Then imagine your breath moving down into your belly, filling it with air like a balloon. Feel your belly gently inflate as you inhale and gently deflate as you exhale. Ideally, you'll feel little movement in the hand on your chest.

When using mindful breathing, you don't have to take full, deep breaths. Instead, focus on taking long, slow breaths with a comfortable rhythm. If you start to feel lightheaded or notice tingling in your lips or fingertips, you're breathing too deeply or too fast. If this happens, breathe naturally, and then try again later.

Read the instructions that follow before beginning the exercise to familiarize yourself with the process. Record the instructions if you'd like to listen to them while you're doing the exercise. Then set an alarm for five minutes and practice mindful breathing until it goes off. After a few weeks of practice, you can set the alarm for longer periods of time, like ten or fifteen minutes. Then, with a few modifications, like keeping your eyes open and not counting, you can begin using mindful breathing in your everyday life, such as when you're driving, doing the dishes, or having a conversation. Whenever you catch yourself being unmindful or getting distracted, use mindful breathing to refocus your attention.

In your diary, note how many times each day you practice mindful breathing.

Instructions: Find a comfortable place to sit or lie down in a room where you won't be disturbed. Begin taking long, slow breaths in through your nose and slowly exhaling through your mouth as though you're blowing out candles. Notice the sensation of your abdomen rising and falling with each breath. (If you'd like, place one hand on your belly to remind yourself to use your diaphragm.) Find a slow, comfortable rhythm of breathing in and out. (If you're making a recording, pause here.)

Now, as you continue to breathe, focus on each breath. Either begin counting your breaths each time you exhale, or simply note to yourself "inhale," then "exhale." You can say these things either silently or aloud. If you're counting each exhalation, do so until you reach four, and then start over at one again. (Pause here.)

When your attention begins to wander and you think of other things, do your best to let go of the thoughts and gently return your focus to your breathing. Notice your abdomen rising and falling with each breath, and continue counting your breaths noting "inhale… exhale…" Try not to criticize yourself for getting distracted. It's natural that you do. Just do your best to stay focused on your breathing.

Keep breathing, focusing your attention, and letting go of distracting thoughts until your alarm goes off. Then slowly return your focus to the room you're in.

Use Wise Mind*

Wise mind (*see card #20 in *The DBT Card Deck*) is the ability to make healthy decisions based on both your emotions and your rational thoughts (Linehan 1993a). Many people who struggle with overwhelming emotions base their decisions solely on how they feel—without considering the facts of a situation—because their emotions are strong and feel like they "must be true." Behaving this way is called using *emotion mind* (Linehan 1993a). Here's an example: "I feel really lonely and depressed, which means I'm a horrible person and I'll be alone for the rest of my life. I should just break up with my boyfriend now, because sooner or later that's what's going to happen anyway." In comparison, some people make decisions based solely on facts and logical thinking, without considering how they feel about their decisions. This is called using *reasonable mind* (Linehan 1993a). Here's an example: "I don't know how I feel about John, but we've been dating for almost a year and we share some common interests, so I guess we should just get married." Obviously, the best way to make healthy decisions is to consider both how you feel and what the facts are; this is called using wise mind.

In order to use wise mind effectively, it's best to relax and focus. Since wise mind is often compared to using your intuition (Linehan 1993b) or making "gut decisions," it's often helpful to focus on the center of your abdomen, the place where it often feels like these decisions originate. The following exercise will help you do that.

Read the instructions that follow before beginning the exercise to familiarize yourself with the process. Record the instructions if you'd like to listen to them while you're doing the exercise. Then set an alarm for five minutes and practice using wise mind until it goes off. Finally, remember that using wise mind takes practice. If answers don't come to you right away, keep trying.

In your diary, note how many times each day you use wise mind.

Instructions: Find a comfortable place to sit or lie down in a room where you won't be disturbed. Begin by placing your hand on the center of your abdomen midway between the bottom of your rib cage and your belly button. This is the center of wise mind. Begin taking long, slow breaths in through your nose and exhaling through your mouth. Notice the sensation of your abdomen rising and falling with each breath and find a slow comfortable rhythm of inhaling and exhaling. As you continue to breathe, let your attention focus on the spot underneath your hand, the center of wise mind. (If you're making a recording, pause here.)

As you continue to focus on the center of wise mind, choose a single problem or decision that you have to make and spend a minute or so thinking about it. What are the facts? What are your feelings about this situation? What are your possible choices? (Pause here.)

As you continue breathing and focusing, ask your center of wise mind for guidance ("What should I do?") just like you'd ask a trusted friend for advice, and then pay attention to any answer you receive. Notice what thoughts or solutions arise out of your center of wise mind. The answer might come in the form of words, pictures, or sounds. Do your best not to judge the answers you receive; just note them to yourself and keep breathing. Notice how the answer or possible solution makes you feel. Notice if it feels right or healthy to you. (Pause here.)

If no thoughts or answers come to you right away, don't worry. Do your best to continue breathing in a mindful way and stay focused on the center of wise mind until your alarm goes off.

Using Wise Mind in Daily Life

After becoming familiar with the preceding exercise, you can start using wise mind to help make decisions in your daily life, even if you can't find the time to be alone. First, breathe and focus your attention on your center of wise mind. Next, think about the decision you're about to make. What are the facts? How do you feel about the situation? What type of decision can you make using wise mind, combining both the facts and your feelings? Then decide on what action you'll take and notice how it feels in your center of wise wind, in your gut. Does it feel right or healthy? If so, go with that decision. If it feels wrong somehow, take some more time to consider both the facts and your feelings before you decide to act. And remember, not all anxiety and nervousness is bad. Sometimes you'll feel nervous when you try something new or difficult; that's natural. Finally, keep track of your decisions and the results—maybe in a notebook—to evaluate if you're using wise mind successfully. When you first start using wise mind, it might be hard to tell if you're making better decisions. The best way to determine this is to look at the results of your decisions and see if you're making healthier choices in your life.

Practice Beginner's Mind*

When you use beginner's mind, you engage in relationships and situations as if you were seeing them for the first time, without any preconceived judgments about how they should be (Suzuki 2001).

Many people who struggle with overwhelming emotions categorize other people and situations into two groups: good and bad. This type of judgment is called black-and-white thinking because it excludes all the shades of gray that exist in between. Whenever you make this type of judgment about someone or something, you limit what you expect and set yourself up for feeling angry, even when you make good judgments. For example, if you're thinking about your best friend and say to yourself, "She will always love me and never betray me," then you'll be easily upset if she doesn't want to spend time with you or says something that you don't agree with. Instead, if you were to simply say, "Today I'll do my best to be mindful with my friend," you won't be constantly comparing her to the standard you've set and therefore won't be so easily disappointed.

The truth is that most people and experiences are a combination of good and bad qualities; no one and nothing is 100 percent good or bad all of the time. Sometimes people do things that make us happy and sometimes they disappoint us. Sometimes situations are pleasing and sometimes they cause frustration, boredom, and emotional pain. A person who uses beginner's mind recognizes this fact and tries to approach each moment of life as if he or she was seeing it for the first time, like an innocent child (*see card #22 in *The DBT Card Deck*).

In your diary, note how many times each day you use beginner's mind.

Instructions: The first step to changing a problem is to recognize when that problem occurs. So to start using beginner's mind you need to recognize when you're making positive and negative judgments. For the next two to three weeks, carry a pen and paper with you and do your best to record any positive or negative judgments that you make about yourself, others, and events as soon as you recognize them. Write down where you were, what was happening, and what the judgment was about. In order to remind yourself to record your judgments, it might help if you give yourself visual reminders, like wearing a special bracelet or writing "judgments" on sticky notes and posting them around your house.

As you continue the practice of recording your judgments, you'll start to catch them soon after you make them. The goal, of course, is to recognize that you're making a judgment as soon as the thought arises, and then let it go. When you recognize that you're making a judgment, you can remind yourself to let it go with a phrase like "Be mindful," "Let go of judgments," or "Use beginner's mind," or a phrase of your own. In addition, you can use mindful breathing to help you let go of judgmental thoughts. If one or more judgmental thoughts keep recurring, try focusing your attention on the rising and falling of your breath or counting your breaths until the judgment disappears. If you need more help, try imagining your judgmental thought floating away on a leaf on a river or drifting away on a cloud in the sky.

Note that beginner's mind is really an extension of using radical acceptance. When you use radical acceptance, you observe situations without judging or criticizing. Beginner's mind requires you to do the same thing with your own thoughts.

Practice Self-Compassion*

To "have compassion" for someone means that you recognize that they are in pain of some kind and need help. Unfortunately, many of us are better at showing compassion to others than we are at being compassionate with ourselves (*see card #26 in *The DBT Card Deck*). Some people think they don't deserve to be helped like other people do because of who they are or what they've done in the past. However, the truth is that you are deserving of compassion, love, and forgiveness just like everyone else.

In fact, practicing self-compassion is really the first step in any type of self-improvement. Making changes in your life is hard, and if you don't believe that you're deserving of kindness, the process can be even harder. No one is perfect, and we've all made mistakes. Self-compassion is the process of applying radical acceptance to who you are right now. None of us can change our pasts, and some of us have made mistakes that we regret, maybe even hurt other people, but each of us is still capable of making positive changes and is deserving of love, happiness, and forgiveness. It all starts with practicing self-compassion. Use the instructions below (adapted from McKay & Wood 2019) to help you. Then, in your diary, note how many times each day you practice self-compassion.

Instructions: Find a comfortable place to sit or lie down where you won't be disturbed for several minutes. With your eyes closed (if comfortable), place one hand on your abdomen and use mindful breathing to help you relax. Slowly breathe in through your nose and allow your abdomen to gently expand like a balloon. Then, even more slowly, breathe out through your mouth allowing your abdomen to gently collapse. As you continue to breathe, begin counting your breaths, either silently or aloud. Count each exhalation from 1 to 4, then begin counting at 1 again. Feel your abdomen slowly rise and fall with each breath. Continue breathing like this for about a minute to develop a slow, steady rhythm. Notice any sensations of peace, calm, or relaxation, and allow them to spread throughout your body.

Now bring your awareness inside your own body, noting any physical or emotional sensations there. Allow yourself to be aware of your breath as it moves through your body giving you life. As you hold that awareness, slowly repeat the following phrases (either silently or aloud) on each exhalation of your breath:

"May I be peaceful."

"May I be safe."

"May I be healthy."

"May I be happy and free from suffering."

Repeat the phrases two or three more times, allowing their meaning to deepen each time. Allow yourself to feel and accept your own sense of compassion.

Finally, when you are done, take a few additional slow breaths, rest quietly, and appreciate your own sense of goodwill and self-compassion.

Use Mindful Communication with Others*

If you notice that your interactions with other people frequently lead to fights, arguments, or not getting what you ask for, it may be that you're not communicating mindfully. *Mindless* communication often sounds like this: "You make me angry," "You did this to me on purpose," or "You're a jerk for not helping me!" In each of these statements, the speaker made a judgment or an accusation toward the person they were addressing. Imagine how you would feel if someone said these things to you. Would you be willing to listen any further or help them with their request? Probably not. These are called mindless "you" statements because they blame the other person ("you") for everything that's happening, and as a result, nothing gets resolved.

In contrast, mindful communication uses "I" statements that often begin with "I think…," "I feel…," or "I want…" (*see card #23 in The DBT Card Deck). These are less threatening to the other person and as a result you are more likely to be heard. Mindful "I" statements are based on how you feel, they are non-judgmental, and they let the other person know the facts of the situation from your perspective.

Let's look at the three mindless "you" statements above and turn them into mindful "I" statements. Instead of "You make me angry," you could say, "Right now, I feel angry." Do you hear the difference? The mindful statement isn't judging anyone, it's just stating a feeling. Instead of saying, "You did this to me on purpose," try saying, "It upsets me that this situation has happened." Again, this isn't blaming the other person, but you're letting the other person know how you feel. Finally, instead of insulting someone and saying "You're a jerk for not helping me," try something like "I'm really upset and angry that I'm not getting the help that I need."

The next time you're in a conversation and need to make a request, state your feelings, or ask someone for help, use mindful "I" statements and you'll be more likely to have your needs met.

In your diary, note how many times each day you use mindful communication with others.

Do What's Effective*

Sometimes in order to reach your goals you have to do the opposite of what you really want to do or something that makes you feel uncomfortable (*see card #24 in The DBT Card Deck). In DBT this is called "doing what's effective" (Linehan 1993b).

Many people who struggle with overwhelming emotions avoid conflict, lash out at others when they don't get what they want, or simply walk out on people and situations that make them upset. But in these situations, their own needs don't get met and the problem is never solved. "Doing what's effective" requires you to put those old habits on hold and choose a more effective coping strategy, even if it makes you feel very uncomfortable. For example, instead of avoiding a conflict maybe you choose to use assertive communication skills even though it makes you feel "pushy." Or instead of lashing out at someone maybe you use radical acceptance, even though it makes you feel like you're "giving in" to the other person. Maybe instead of walking out on someone who is making you angry you assess the feelings-threat balance before coping (FTB-Cope), even though it doesn't feel like "the right thing to do."

Doing what's effective is a mindfulness skill because it requires you to be aware of what's happening in the present moment so you can choose to do something that will achieve your goal—in spite of how you might *feel*—rather than simply reacting without thinking. Doing what's effective also requires you to be mindful of any judgments you have about yourself, others, or the situation, which might prevent you from achieving your goals. For example, you might think that someone is "rude" or the situation is "unfair," but if you are mindful of these judgments, you can use your coping skills and do what's effective anyway.

There's an old saying that goes "fake it till you make it," meaning do what's necessary even if it feels uncomfortable and you don't want to do it. The same applies to doing what's effective. Remember, to reach your goals you have to be able and willing to do things that make you feel uncomfortable sometimes. So, to do what's effective, remember to:

- Be mindful of your thoughts and feelings

- Avoid judging yourself, others, or the situation

- Use coping skills that will help you achieve your goals

- Do the best you can even if you don't feel like doing anything

In your diary, note how many times each day you did what was effective.

Complete a Task Mindfully*

As you continue to practice your mindfulness skills, you should begin to use them in your everyday life. Throughout the day check the way you're breathing and do a few minutes of mindful breathing. Then, note how you're feeling and what you're thinking. Similarly, do your best to be mindful of your actions and complete as many tasks as mindfully as you can (*see card #25 in *The DBT Card Deck*).

For example, if you're driving to work, notice what you're thinking about—maybe what you have to do once you get to work. Notice what you're hearing, perhaps the radio or the other cars in traffic. Next, check in with how you're sitting and the way you're holding your body. Notice how you're feeling emotionally and physically, maybe anxious and tired. If you're eating or drinking something, notice what that tastes like. There's no exact order; just do your best to focus and shift your attention between your thoughts, feelings, physical sensations, and actions in order to be mindful of your present-moment experience.

If you notice something that's bothering you, do your best to let it go. For example, if you notice that you're breathing in a short, shallow way, use mindful breathing. If you notice that your shoulders are tight and hunched, let go of the tension and allow your shoulders to drop. If you recognize that you're not paying attention to the road, shift your focus to your driving. If you're having a judgmental thought, let it go. If you're eating or drinking something that doesn't taste good, stop.

In your diary, note how many times each day you complete a task mindfully.

Instructions: A helpful way to practice completing tasks mindfully is to start with smaller tasks and work your way up to more difficult ones. Here's an example of a stepwise progression:

- *Walk mindfully.* Notice how your body balances and how each foot rolls from heel to toe with each step.

- *Eat something mindfully.* Start by noticing the texture of the food, then notice what it tastes like and how it feels to chew it slowly and swallow it.

- *Wash the dishes by hand mindfully.* Feel the soap and water on your hands and notice the way you scrub and the sound of the water.

- *Complete a work task or school assignment mindfully.* Observe what you're thinking, feeling, and doing while you complete the task. Pay attention to your breathing.

- *Have a mindful communication with someone.* Breathe mindfully while listening, use beginner's mind to let go of judgments, and use wise mind to make any decisions.

CHAPTER 3

Emotion Regulation

Emotion regulation skills are the cornerstone for a happier life. They make a large differ-ence in how you respond to challenging situations and how others respond to you. Here are eight key emotion regulation skills:

- Engage in physical regulation

- Balance thoughts and feelings

- Plan positive events

- Name and let go of thoughts

- Name and observe emotions

- Don't act on emotions

- Act the opposite of your urges

- Use problem solving

Engage in Physical Regulation*

The first step toward emotion regulation has nothing to do with emotions. Rather, it's about physical regulation (*see card #30 in *The DBT Card Deck*). The reason it's so important is this: When your body is in an unhealthy state, the resulting physical distress can cause emotional vulnerability. In other words, when you're physically stressed, emo-tional distress won't be far behind.

Treat Pain or Illness

Everyone knows a headache will make you irritable, and chronic physical pain or illness will do worse than that. If you sometimes experience overwhelming emotions, it's imperative that you find a way to treat or manage pain. Don't wait for pain or illness to trigger emotional instability—get help right away. Get diagnosed and develop a specific plan to manage your symptoms.

In your diary, note how many times each day you're able to cope with pain, and record what strategies you used in the "NOTES" column.

Balance Your Eating

Both the amount and types of food you eat can trigger emotional instability. Here are some guidelines on how to eat in a more balanced way:

- Avoid a lot of sugar. High-sugar foods (soft drinks, candy, cakes, pastries, and so on) cause a huge elevation in blood sugar that makes you excited but then irritable, anxious, and depressed as it wears off.

- Avoid large amounts of fat (fried food, sausage, and so on) because these often trigger feelings of heaviness, lethargy, and depression.

- Avoid caffeine as much as possible (coffee, tea, colas, chocolate, and so on) because these make you more likely to get angry or react with anxiety. And when the caffeine wears off, it can leave you feeling tired and down.

- Don't skip meals. When you do, it causes blood sugar levels to fall and creates a hypoglycemic state, making you vulnerable and anxious.

- Eat moderate portions. Overeating acts initially as a tranquilizer, then pushes you toward lethargy and depression.

- Eat whole grains, vegetables, fruits, and protein every day.

- Without balanced nutrition, you'll feel less well and more emotionally vulnerable.

In your diary, note how many times each day you eat in a balanced way.

Avoid Drugs and Alcohol

Alcohol and drugs give you a temporary lift. But the problem is in that word "temporary." All drugs and alcohol have secondary effects that soon obscure the good ones. Every substance, as you start to come down from it, will tend to irritate and depress you and push you deeper into the hole you were trying to climb out of—which is likely to make you want to take some more to try to feel better again. This Jekyll-and-Hyde aspect of drugs and alcohol, trapping you on an endless up-and-down seesaw, makes you vulnerable to wild swings of emotion. You'll feel good one minute, then bad the next.

Don't do drugs or alcohol to fix emotional storms—they will only get worse. If you feel the least bit fragile, stay away; your vulnerability will only intensify. You're reading this book because your emotions get overwhelming at times. Because of secondary effects, we strongly urge you not to use drugs. And the rule for alcohol should be one drink or none at all.

In your diary, note each day that you avoid using drugs or alcohol.

Get Sufficient Sleep

Perhaps there is nothing more unbalancing to your emotional life than sleep problems. Whether you have difficulties with getting to sleep or you wake up during the night, these problems *must* be addressed if you are to achieve emotion regulation. Your physician may suggest a medication such as trazodone or a drug in the class known as hypnotics to help regulate your sleep. Your physician may also describe a program of sleep hygiene in which you develop habits that facilitate sleep, including the following:

- Avoid caffeine, nicotine, and alcohol in the evening. Also avoid exercise and stimulating TV programs late at night.

- Avoid napping during the day.

- Go to bed *at the same time* and get up *at the same time* every day, even on weekends.

- Use your bed for sleeping and sex only. Don't read or watch TV or do any kind of work in bed.

- If you can't fall asleep within twenty minutes or if you awaken and lie sleepless for more than twenty minutes, *get out of bed.* Read or do something nonstimulating. When you get sleepy, go back to bed. If twenty minutes goes by and you're still awake, repeat the process.

In your diary, note any day you get sufficient sleep.

Get Regular Exercise

Getting twenty to thirty minutes of exercise on most days can be more effective than the best antidepressants for lifting your mood. It also helps reduce anxiety and anger reactions because exercise releases endorphins—hormones that relax and calm you. It doesn't really matter what kind of exercise you do—walking, jogging, bicycling, rowing, swimming, weight training, or whatever. You just have to do it regularly to achieve the emotion regulation effects.

In your diary, note any day you do at least twenty minutes of exercise.

Balance Your Thoughts and Feelings*

Sometimes when you get overwhelmed by an experience you fail to look at the "big picture" and miss important details (*see card #34 in *The DBT Card Deck*). For example, maybe your girlfriend has told you how happy she is to be with you, but when she disagrees with something you say, you think she's planning to leave you. Or maybe at work you've always received excellent performance reviews, but one day your boss passes you without saying hello and you suddenly become worried you are going to be fired. This type of misinterpretation is called "filtering" (Beck, Rush, Shaw, & Emery 1979), and it's like wearing a pair of sunglasses that blocks out positive details in your life and only lets you see the negative ones. None of your accomplishments are ever good enough. Compliments from other people don't count. And you're always worried that somebody is going to abandon you—even if they say that they're not. Living your life this way creates anxiety, fear, and dissatisfaction because nothing is ever going to be good enough when you expect everything to go wrong.

In order to balance your thoughts—and therefore your feelings—you need to practice looking at all the evidence of a situation when your negative emotions get triggered:

- Evidence that you're doing well versus your self-critical thoughts

- Evidence that good things can happen versus your fear that everything turns bad

- Evidence that people like you versus your negative beliefs that they don't

The opposite of filtering is "seeing the big picture," and it requires you to pause and consider all the evidence before jumping to a negative conclusion. This can be difficult to do at first. Many people who struggle with overwhelming emotions habitually go straight to negative thoughts without even considering a positive option. So seeing the big picture—meaning *all* the evidence, good and bad—will probably take some practice before it feels natural. But the more you do it, the better you'll get at noticing the positive in your life. And the more positivity you notice, the more likely you are to start feeling more positive too.

To see the big picture and balance positive thoughts with your negative thoughts, practice asking yourself the following questions the next time a situation makes you frustrated, scared, or angry:

1. What happened? What are the facts—positive and negative?

2. How did the situation make you feel? (This is the negative feeling, but try to be specific.)

3. What evidence *supports* how you feel? (These are the negative things you usually notice that make you feel bad.)

4. What evidence *contradicts* how you feel? (These are the positive facts you usually overlook, that might make you feel better if you noticed them.)

5. Putting together the evidence that both *supports* and *contradicts* how you felt originally, what's a more balanced way of seeing all the facts of this situation? How does seeing the bigger picture make you feel?

6. Now seeing the big picture, what's a healthier way of coping with this situation?

To practice seeing the big picture, think back to a few recent situations that made you upset or angry and ask yourself the questions above. Do your best to consider all the evidence and find more balanced thoughts and feelings, as well as a healthier way to have coped with the situation. Keep practicing until you can remember the six questions. Then, the next time you experience a situation that upsets you, do your best to ask yourself those questions before you react as you usually do. In your diary, note how many times each day you balance your thoughts and feelings.

Plan Positive Events*

Plan a minimum of one positive event for each day (*see card #35 in *The DBT Card Deck*). Having a healthy emotional life means you have to balance some of the negative and challenging experiences everyone faces with positive ones. Each morning when you wake up, identify one positive event that you can look forward to that day. This might be phoning or visiting a friend, doing something interesting or meaningful, enjoying a sport or hobby, or enjoying a soothing experience like listening to a new CD or taking a long bath. It might even be getting something done that will improve your life.

Planning one positive event a day is good. Two is better. Three is even better for emotional balance.

In your diary, note the number of positive events you engage in each day, and record what the events were in the "NOTES" column.

Name and Let Go of Thoughts*

There are two kinds of thoughts that are likely to produce overwhelming emotions—judgmental thoughts (about yourself or others) and catastrophic thoughts (about bad things that might happen). Judgmental thoughts are the royal road to depression when they're turned on yourself, and they'll stoke anger when focused on someone else. Catastrophic thoughts that focus on future distress or danger often drive feelings of anxiety. There's a simple process for not getting embroiled in this painful thinking (*see card #36 in *The DBT Card Deck*):

1. Name the thought. Say to yourself, "There's a judgment" or "There's a scary thought" or simply "That's a thought." With that, you don't have to get involved in it or believe it. It's just a thought, not a fact; just something your mind says, not reality.

2. Take a breath, and as you let go of the breath, you can let go of the thought.

3. Visualize the thought drifting away—like a leaf down a stream, like a car down a road, like a deer jumping into a thicket. Just let it go, and when the next judgment or scary thought comes, do the same thing.

In your diary, note how many times each day you're able to name and let go of thoughts.

Name and Observe Emotions*

It's important not to run from what you feel. The more you try to avoid emotions, the stronger and more insistent they become. Then they sometimes feel like they're overwhelming you to a point where you might do something dangerous or impulsive. It's a paradox: The more you try to control what you feel, the more it ends up controlling you.

There are two things you can do to escape this dilemma. The first is to always name what you feel. Finding words for emotions helps you say and face what you fear. Verbalizing makes feelings less overwhelming and more understandable. Chapter 4 has a list of emotions in the section "Knowing What You Want." You can look for descriptive words there. The more precisely and clearly you can describe what you feel, the less overwhelmed you'll be (*see card #37 in *The DBT Card Deck*).

Another good way to deal with strong feelings is to observe them. All feelings come like waves. They grow for a while, then they peak, and finally they slide back to a calmer, quieter place. Observing your feelings is sometimes called *emotion exposure*. Here's how you do it:

1. Name the feeling.

2. Describe (out loud or silently to yourself) everything about the feeling. Describe its intensity; notice if there are other emotions woven into it.

3. Note where you feel it in your body. What is that feeling like? How hot or cold is it? Remember, it's a wave, so pay attention to any changes in intensity—either increasing or decreasing.

4. Describe the emotion as a color, a shape, or a texture if that seems appropriate.

5. Notice if the feeling starts to change into another emotion.
   For example, anger often shifts into sadness, and vice versa.

6. Throughout emotion exposure, as thoughts show up, name and let them go.

After the wave has diminished or shifted to some other feeling, you can stop watching and describing if you want. But the next time a strong emotion shows up, we suggest you do the same thing: name, describe, and watch the wave.

Occasionally, as you observe an emotion, it will seem to only grow bigger. If you get exhausted, that's okay. You've done enough. It's fine to stop observing and instead use distraction, self-soothing, relaxation, or other skills from chapter 1, on distress tolerance, to let things subside.

So to summarize the process, when a significant emotion shows up, name it and watch it. Usually the wave will diminish. If it doesn't, use distress tolerance skills to soothe yourself.

In your diary, note how many times each day you're able to name and watch an emotion.

Don't Act on Emotions

Your emotions and your behavior are strongly linked. Every emotion triggers what's called an action urge. When you're anxious, the urge is typically to avoid or retreat. When you're ashamed, the impulse is to hide or defend yourself. When you're sad, you feel the need to shut down and cease activity. When you're angry, you have the urge to attack or fight. Many painful emotions are also accompanied by an impulse to numb and block the pain. Using drugs, engaging in self-mutilating behaviors, bingeing, and other numbing strategies are all driven by an action urge to stop the feeling, no matter how.

One problem with action urges is that they negatively affect relationships, the ability to work competently, and your general happiness. Another difficulty is that they often feel automatic—like you have to do whatever your emotion pushes you to do. But this isn't the case. While it's often true that you have no choice about a feeling showing up, you do have the ability to choose how you'll respond to it. Your behavior *is* under your control.

On a piece of paper, write down the action urges that get you in trouble—things that alienate others or undermine the quality of your life. You can organize the list by first looking at key emotions (anger, sadness, shame, guilt, fear, or anxiety), and then listing problem behaviors you do in response. Next, circle the action urges you most want to change. What people and situations tend to trigger them? Write these down next to the circled urges. These are the situations you need to watch for, and then when you encounter them, resist the urges that go with them.

In your diary, note how many times each day you're able to *not* respond to one of these urges.

Act the Opposite of Your Urges*

There's more you can do with action urges than just resist them. You can behave exactly the opposite from what the urge pushes you to do (*see card #38 in *The DBT Card Deck*). While acting on urges tends to intensify and prolong painful emotions, acting the opposite helps regulate them. It often changes the emotion into something softer and more positive.

Acting the opposite involves changing your voice, posture, words, and actions to conform with an emotion that's diametrically opposed to what you actually feel. Here's what it looks like:

Emotion	Action Urge	Opposite Action
Anger	Attack, hurt, shout, point	Validate, speak in a soft voice, adopt a relaxed posture
Fear	Avoid, hunch, speak in a high voice	Approach what you fear, do what you've been avoiding, stand tall, speak in a calm voice
Sadness	Sit down, be passive, slump, speak in a weak voice	Be active, get involved, stand straight, speak in a strong voice
Guilt and shame	Hide, avoid, shut down, slump, speak in a high voice	If appropriate, atone, make amends, stand straight, speak in a strong voice

To put opposite action into effect, you can do the following:

1. Using the list of action urges that get you into trouble (from the previous section), select three where you seriously want to implement opposite action.

2. Identify the voice, posture, words, and actions you use when acting on these three urges.

3. Identify the opposite action. How would you change your voice, posture, words, or behavior to fit with an opposite response?

4. Fully commit to opposite action in the situations the trigger these three urges. Keep in mind why you want to regulate these emotions and change the problematic action urges. Try to stay aware of the costs—to you and others—of the associated emotion-driven behaviors.

5. Monitor for emotions and situations where you want to make this change. Then implement your plan. Opposite action literally sends a message to the brain that the old emotion is no longer appropriate and helps you shift away from it.

In your diary, note how many times each day you practice opposite action.

Use Problem Solving*

Problem solving starts with problem analysis (sometimes called behavior analysis). Behavior analysis is necessary because you can't solve a problem you don't understand. Every time you react because of an action urge in a way that creates upset or turmoil, you should explore exactly what happened (*see card #39 in *The DBT Card Deck*). For example, what happened just before the problem emotion and behavior took place? In other words, what was the triggering event? Did you do anything to contribute to that triggering event? Keep examining the situation as it unfolded and write down what happened after the event:

- What were your immediate thoughts after the event?

- How did you feel right after the event?

- What did you do right after the event?

As other people responded to you or you responded to your own actions, you may have gone through additional cycles of thoughts, feelings, and behaviors. Try to write down as much of this as you remember.

Now comes the problem-solving process. When you look at each unfolding step in the sequence—your thoughts, feelings, and behaviors—what might you have done differently? To help you come up with solutions, make a list of the following alternative responses:

- Coping thoughts you might have used

- Self-soothing, relaxation, or other distress tolerance skills (from chapter 1) that might have calmed you emotionally

- Mindfulness skills (from chapter 2) that would have helped you focus

- Opposite actions you could have substituted for action urges

- Healthier behavioral responses (covered in chapter 4) that could have turned the situation around

Write down all of your responses. The more ideas you can generate the better. Then choose the best ideas you've come up with. Narrow the list down to somewhere between one and three of the best alternative coping responses. Then commit to using your new ideas when similar situations present themselves in the future. If you have predictable situations, identify specific times and places where you'll try your new responses.

Because problem solving is so important to emotion regulation, in your diary use a star to indicate how many times each day you're able to engage in a problem-solving process.

CHAPTER 4

Interpersonal Effectiveness

Interpersonal skills can make an enormous difference in your relationships and in your life. They are the cornerstone of effective communication and will help you get along with others, get what you need, and solve problems. This chapter focuses on six key interpersonal skills:

- Practice compassion for others

- Make assertive requests

- Say no assertively

- Negotiate agreements

- Listen to and understand others

- Validate others

Perhaps the most crucial of these skills is the assertive request, because the ability to ask for things is foundational to keeping a healthy give-and-take balance in your relationships.

Practice Compassion for Others*

Everyone experiences pain and disappointment in life, it's unavoidable. In fact, one of the basic tenets of Buddhist philosophy is that all people suffer. This doesn't mean you will suffer *all the time*, but it does mean that it cannot be avoided—it will happen. Even the wealthiest and most successful people experience heartache, sadness, and pain at times.

All of us suffer, and as human beings, we all deserve compassion and kindness to help with our struggles (*see card #52 in *The DBT Card Deck*).

This is often easy to remember with people we care about, but difficult to remember when other people make us angry, don't give us what we want, or make our lives more difficult in some way. We frequently become angry, resentful, or judgmental about the other person, forgetting that they might be suffering too in some way that is unknown to us. Over the course of our lifetime, resentments and judgments about others can certainly build up to a toxic level and influence how we think and the way we interact with other people.

Imagine what could happen if you instead practiced compassion for others—even compassion for people you've never met and people you don't even like. Rather than building up toxic levels of resentment you can let go of judgments, find a new way to connect with people through acceptance and kindness, remain calmer and more peaceful, and choose healthier coping strategies when faced with a moment of choice. Use Other-Compassion Meditation (adapted from McKay & Wood 2019) to develop understanding, kindness, and caring for others. Then, in your diary, note how many times each day you practice compassion for others.

Instructions: To begin, use mindful breathing to help yourself relax. Find a comfortable place to sit or lie down where you won't be disturbed. Begin taking slow breaths in through your nose and exhaling through your mouth. Find a slow steady rhythm and let yourself relax. Feel your abdomen rise as you inhale and gently deflate as you exhale. Do your best to stay focused on the rising and falling of your breath for a few minutes. Try counting your inhalations from "1" to "4," and then start over at "1" again. Now bring your awareness to your body and note any sensations of peace or calm and allow those sensations to spread throughout your body.

Then, when you feel at least moderately relaxed and focused, think of someone who makes you smile, someone who naturally makes you feel happy. (Pause here.) Note how this person makes you feel both physically and emotionally when you're with them. (Pause here.) Now recognize that this person also wants to be happy and free of suffering. As you hold that awareness, send good intentions to that person by stating (silently or aloud):

"May you be peaceful."

"May you be safe."

"Maybe you be healthy."

"Maybe you be happy and free of suffering."

Repeat the phrases two or three more times, allowing their meaning to deepen within you and allowing yourself to feel a more meaningful sensation of compassion for that person.

Now, call to mind the image of someone you dislike or find difficult. Remember that this person is also struggling in life in many ways you cannot know, and that they are likely doing the best they can too and may not even be aware of the pain they are causing you. Do your best to extend your compassion to this person, acknowledge their humanity, and release any judgments you may be holding. Send your best intentions to this person (silently or aloud):

"Just as I want to be peaceful and free from suffering… May you, too, find peace."

"May you be safe."

"May you be healthy."

"May you be happy and free from suffering."

Again, repeat the phrases two or three more times, allowing their meaning to deepen within you. Do your best to find even a small bit of compassion for this person that you find difficult.

When you have completed the meditation instructions, take a few more slow breaths and allow yourself to feel the sensations of compassion that you extended to these people. As you continue to practice in private, try silently extending compassion to people as you meet them. Try thinking to yourself, "Just like me, this person wants to be happy and free of suffering." Or, "Just like me, these people are doing the best they can to cope with the drama of their lives." Do your best to extend compassion to all persons that you meet and notice how it changes your interactions with them.

Make Assertive Requests*

Before you can ask for anything, you have to know what you want (*see cards #44, 45, 46, and 47 in *The DBT Card Deck*). Many of us have grown up in families where children were discouraged from expressing, or even knowing, their needs. It may have felt dangerous to want or ask for much because the adults in your life got angry or were disapproving. Now, years later, it may feel difficult to even seek words for what you need. Perhaps you hold back, waiting for things to somehow get better. And when they don't, you're likely to explode with pent-up pain and frustration.

Knowing What You Want

Knowing what you want starts with identifying the painful feeling you're having in the context of a particular relationship. Recall a recent upsetting interaction. Actively visualize what was going on and pay attention to your emotional experience. Now try to find a word for it among the following choices:

afraid	empty	pushed
alone	exhausted	rejected
angry	foolish	sad
annoyed	forgotten	stressed
anxious	frustrated	tired
ashamed	hopeless	unappreciated
away	hurt	uncared for
bored	insecure	uncomfortable
depleted	irritated	unnoticed
depressed	left out	unrecognized
deprived	lost	upset
disappointed	neglected	vulnerable
disrespected	nervous	worried
disturbed	overwhelmed	
embarrassed	overworked	

When you've found the word that describes your emotion, write it down. A simple way to phrase it is "When _____happened, I felt _____."

The next step is clarifying what you want the other person to change—what you want more of or less of, or what you want the other person to start doing or stop doing. You might also include where or when you want this change to occur. Notice that you are asking for a *behavioral* change—not for a change in feelings or attitude. Now write this request down in one or two simple sentences.

Saying What You Want

An assertive request has four parts: saying what you *think* the problem is, stating what you *feel* about the situation, identifying what you *want* specifically and behaviorally, and describing your *self-care solution*—how you plan to take care of yourself if the other person won't cooperate. Let's examine each component.

"I think." This is where you try to describe the facts of the situation without blaming or judging. It's a clear, specific, non-attacking recital of the problem as you understand it. Here are two examples: "Twice this week, when it was your turn to do the dishes, you didn't do them until the next night" and "When you get home these days, you most often spend time with e-mail or the Internet."

"I feel." This is where you describe your emotional reaction to the problem. While you might leave this component out with a store clerk or repair person, it's important information for anyone who knows and cares about you. Statements about feelings never begin "I feel *that*...," because this is actually the start of an opinion, not your feelings. Here are two examples of stating how you really feel: "I feel irritated" and "I feel alone and unnoticed."

"I want." This component is your opportunity to ask for something. Again, you're more likely to succeed if you request something specific and behavioral. It's also helpful to ask for *one change at a time*. Loading on multiple requests may overwhelm the other person. Here are two examples: "I'd like the dishes to be done in the evening so I don't have to look at them in the morning" and "When you come home, I'd like you to spend fifteen to twenty minutes checking in about my day and telling me about yours."

Self-care solution. This is an optional component of an assertive request. You can use it to encourage or reinforce people who typically don't pay attention to your needs. The self-care solution describes what you'll do to meet your own needs if the other person isn't willing to work with you. Here are two examples: "If you can't get the dishes done, I'm going to stop cooking dinner in a dirty kitchen" and "If we can't spend time together when you get home, I'm going to take some evening classes and do things with friends so I won't feel so alone."

An assertive request is best prepared in advance. Write out each *I think*, *I feel*, and *I want* component in a brief script, then add a self-care solution if the situation calls for it. The more you think through what exactly you're going to say (perhaps even practicing a few times to hear how it sounds), the more likely you'll succeed with your assertive request. Preparing for highly stressful situations or difficult people may require even more advance work. In such cases, you may want to rehearse a bit with someone you trust, perhaps having them role-play the other person.

Dealing with Resistance

When you make an assertive request, sometimes the other person will start arguing with you about the facts of the situation or try to undermine the legitimacy of what you want. Don't get drawn into this. Your feelings aren't debatable, nor are your wants. Simply repeat your request (perhaps using slightly different words) in what's called the *broken record technique*. Validate that the other person may have his or her own experience and needs, but return again and again to a simple statement of what you would like changed. Here are two examples: "I do appreciate that you feel tired in the evening, but I find seeing dishes in the morning irritating and would like them done the night before" and "I see how you need some time to decompress when you first get home, but I'd still like to spend the first fifteen to twenty minutes reconnecting before you head for your computer."

In your diary, note how many times each day you make an assertive request.

Say No Assertively*

An individual who can't say no or set limits relinquishes control to other people. Getting into a relationship where you can't say no is like getting in a car without any brakes. It's dangerous, and sooner or later you're going to crash.

There are only two steps to saying no: validate the other person's need or desire, and then state a clear preference not to do it. If appropriate, you may also include information about what motivates your preference, such as a feeling or situation that's affecting you (*see card #49 in *The DBT Card Deck*). Here are some examples:

- "I know it would be fun for you to go camping this weekend, but I'm really tired and would prefer to rest."

- "I know you love French films, but I don't want to struggle with subtitles tonight."

- "I know you find risky sex exciting, but it triggers very uncomfortable feelings for me, and I would rather not."

- "This apartment does have the view you're looking for, but for me it's too dark. I couldn't live here."

- "I know you'd like to drive together, but I prefer to leave the party when I want. I'll take my own car."

- "That's a fun and tempting invitation, but I need to say no tonight."

As with assertive requests, saying no tends to have a better outcome when you plan what you're going to say. Here are the steps:

1. Write out your script. Validate the other person's need and then state your preference.

2. Rehearse your script out loud or role-play with someone you trust.

3. Decide exactly when and where you'll use your assertive statement.

4. Commit to doing it.

In your diary, note how many times each day you say no in an assertive way.

Negotiate Agreements*

When you've made an assertive request or tried to set a limit and the other person has a strong and different preference, you'll need to negotiate (*see card #51 in *The DBT Card Deck*). Use the VASE acronym to stay on track:

- **V**alidate the other person's need or concern. Then, in a non-attacking way, contrast it with your own.

- **A**sk the other person for a compromise solution that incorporates both your needs.

- **S**uggest alternatives if the first compromise doesn't work for you. Remember that you should try to work both of your needs into a compromise for it to succeed. Each of you should take turns making suggestions until something feels right to both of you.

- **E**xpress yourself in a neutral voice, without anger or contempt.

Notice that the VASE acronym starts with validation. Appreciating the other person's point of view is the best way to disarm the person and enlist his or her cooperation. Then you invite the other person to make a suggestion. If you make the first suggestion, the other person is likely to resist and argue against your solution. Only after the other person has made a proposal should you offer suggestions of your own. Always keep your voice and demeanor calm, with no hint of distress or negative emotion. Remember, a VASE is a beautiful thing that requires careful handling, just like a successful negotiation.

In your diary, note how many times each day you use negotiation skills.

Listen to and Understand Others*

Listening is an active, not passive, process. And without active listening, communication falls apart. Listening requires a full commitment to really understanding the other person's needs, feelings, and point of view. The same things you must understand about yourself to make an assertive request (what you think, feel, and want) are exactly what you need to learn about the other person (*see card #48 in *The DBT Card Deck*). To hear and understand others, you have to do two things:

- You need to stop talking and stop preparing your next comment. And while you're being quiet, you need to listen and remember what the other person is saying.

- You should ask questions to clarify the other person's experience. Here are some recommended questions:

- "What's the problem as you understand it?"

- "What are your feelings about the situation?"

- "Is there something you're afraid will happen here?"

- "What do you want or need in this situation?"

- "What's your idea about the best outcome or resolution?"

Notice that these questions are all designed to elicit critical information so you'll know what you're dealing with. The greatest problem we encounter in all relationships is not understanding what's going on. In these cases, the other person remains a bit of a mystery and we just don't get what they feel or what motivates them. How they see the world remains unknown to us, so we keep failing as we attempt to solve problems. Think back to the last several conflicts you've had with others and try to remember if you learned their perspectives, feelings, and needs. If you didn't, resolve to ask those questions next time.

The basic skill of listening is about getting inside the other person's skin—inside their head. But there are things that can get in your way. Here are some blocks to active listening:

- *Pouncing:* finding something you disagree with and jumping all over it

- *Rehearsing:* planning what you want to say next

- *Filtering:* listening only to things that are important and relevant to you, while ignoring the rest (including what's important to the other person)

- *Judging:* evaluating the other person rather than trying to understand

- *Mind reading:* assuming you know what the other person needs and feels

- *Needing to be right:* resisting anything that suggests you might be wrong or should change

Watch for these listening blocks whenever you're in a disagreement with someone. Or think back over the conversation and see which blocks got in the way of truly understanding the other person's experience.

In your diary, note how many times each day you use your listening and understanding skills.

Validate Others*

Validation doesn't mean you simply agree with the other person. It also doesn't mean you don't advocate for your own point of view. It just means you've listened to and acknowledged what the other person said (*see card #51 in *The DBT Card Deck*). Without validation, people feel unheard, so they redouble their efforts to convince you of the legitimacy of their needs. As they feel more desperate to be heard, they may get loud, trying to overpower you. And you may become loud in return, escalating so you can stand your ground.

Validation starts with this premise: In a conflict, both you and the other person have *equally valid needs.* They aren't the same needs, and they may be supported by hugely different viewpoints, but both are valid. This means you are each entitled to want and feel what you do. Neither is wrong, and neither is right. You just have different—yet reasonable and understandable—experiences and wishes.

To validate someone's needs or experience, you can use a technique called *active listening*. Here's how it works: Just say back what you've heard, in your own words. Try to be accurate, and don't put any slant on it that supports your own point of view. Avoid any sarcasm or suggestion that there's something foolish or wrong in the other person's experience.

When doing active listening, try to remember and report each of the major points you heard. Don't focus on one issue and ignore others. Pay attention to and summarize any statement that indicates how the other person feels, or what he or she wants. Doing this in regard to feelings and needs has a greater validation effect than anything else you could say. Here are some examples:

- "I hear you, it's irritating to see the dirty dishes in the morning. You want them done before then."

- "If I'm understanding right, you're feeling alone and ignored when I get home and jump on the computer. You'd rather we spend some time connecting first."

Sometimes you can combine validation with a reminder of your own position or need. This is called mutual validation, and it looks like this:

- "I understand that you're worried about our line of credit debt and want to start paying it down as soon as possible. On my end, doing some capital investing in new equipment would position us well as orders pick up. Let's put our heads together and try to figure this out."

- "I understand you feel hurt and bored when I'm late. I would, too. On my end, our visits always seem timed in such a way that I have to leave work early and face commuter traffic. Let's put our heads together to figure something out."

In your diary, note how many times each day you use your validation skills.

CHAPTER 5

Exposure-Based Cognitive Rehearsal

To cope with problematic situations while you are upset or angry, it's often helpful to practice your coping skills while you are in a state of slightly heightened emotion. This type of practice is modeled on a research-based phenomena called *state-dependent learning*, which has shown that your emotions play a role in your ability to recall information (Weingartner, Miller, & Murphy 1977; Bower 1981; Szymanski & O'Donohue 1995; Nutt & Lam 2011). For example, information you learned in a relaxed environment is more likely to be recalled in an equally relaxed environment. However, coping skills are often learned in a relaxed environment but, as is the case with DBT and overwhelming emotions, the times when you need to use them are when you're anxious or angry. For help during difficult times, you'll need to practice *exposure-based cognitive rehearsal (EBCR)*.

EBCR is the technique of using your imagination to recreate a troubling situation—along with the emotion you were feeling—and then using one of your many DBT coping skills to handle the emotion in a new, healthier way. Use the following steps to practice EBCR (McKay & West 2016):

1. Select an emotion coping skill that you want to practice, but make sure that you're already familiar with the skill and how to use it. For example, you might choose one of these emotion coping skills or one of many others:

    *   Radical acceptance

    *   Self-soothing

    *   Mindful breathing

    *   Problem solving

    *   Wise mind

2. Next, think of a real situation that has occurred in your life during which you could have used that coping skill. Pick a situation that is vivid enough for you to remember the details and which also evokes a moderate amount of emotion when you recall it.

3. Now visualize the troubling situation in as much detail as you can recall. Imagine the setting, the other people involved, the problems that bothered you, what was said, and even how the situation made you feel. Continue visualizing all the details until you start to feel a moderate-level of troubling emotion. Also pay attention to your body and where you feel the emotion.

4. As you imagine the scene, rate your emotional level of intensity, from 0 (no emotion) to 10 (the worst you can possibly feel). Keep imagining the details until your emotion rises to about a 5, a moderate level of discomfort, then stop the imaginal recall process.

5. Now, begin using the coping skill that you chose at the beginning of the exercise. Put your focus on using the skill and soothing your emotion. Don't try to recall further details of the memory at this point. Keep coping until you feel your emotional intensity drop down 2 or 3 points.

6. Once you notice your emotional intensity dropping a few points, go back and repeat steps 3, 4, and 5. Re-imagine the scene again, notice your emotions rising, and then cope again until you notice a drop in emotional intensity.

The more you practice coping with an emotionally-charged memory, the more easily you will be able to remember that coping skill in the future. Practice each skill with different emotionally-charged memories. The more successful practice you have, the more confident you'll feel using those skills in the future. You can also imagine emotionally-charged events that you know you will have to confront *in the future*. Then go through the same process of selecting an appropriate coping skill, imagining the future scene and any emotions it is likely to bring up, and then practice coping. Again, the more prepared you are to confront the future event, the more confident you will be that you can cope with it.

In your diary, note how many times each day you practice EBCR.

Conclusion

Dialectical behavior therapy is an excellent treatment for people who are struggling with overwhelming emotions and other problems. However, it's only effective if you use the skills every day; just reading about them isn't enough.

Hopefully, you've already had some success using the skills in this book. Maybe you've learned how to distract yourself instead of cutting, reconnected with your higher power, learned how to relax, used wise mind to make decisions, acted the opposite of your urges, or made assertive requests to get your needs met. The key to continued recovery is to keep using the skills that work for you.

However, if you find that you're stuck, feeling hopeless, or just can't seem to change your old habits, think about why you're doing this work in the first place. In other words, what's motivating you to change? Go back to the section "Commit to Valued Action," in chapter 1, and think about the new life you're trying to create for yourself. What do you want that life to look like in the near future? How will you be different? How will your life be better? What types of relationships do you want to have? If you can, use your imagination to create a mental image of you succeeding in the future and doing the things you want to do; then remember that image every time you feel stuck or hopeless. Remind yourself why you're working so hard. Success might be difficult, but it's not impossible. Keep using your DBT skills every day, and you're sure to see improvements.

And remember, if at any point you have too hard a time implementing the skills, please consult a qualified DBT therapist.

Diary

WEEK 1.

Core Skills	Coping Strategies	M	T	W
Distress Tolerance	Stopped Self-Destructive Action			
	Used the REST Strategy			
	Used Radical Acceptance			
	Distracted from Pain			
	Engaged in Pleasurable Activities			
	Soothed Myself			
	Practiced Relaxation			
	Committed to Valued Action			
	Rehearsed Values-Based Behavior			
	Connected with My Higher Power			
	Used Coping Thoughts			
	Determined Feelings-Threat Balance			
	Used Coping Strategies			
	Used Physiological-Coping Skills			
Mindfulness	Practiced Mindful Breathing			
	Used Wise Mind			
	Practiced Beginner's Mind			
	Practiced Self-Compassion			
	Used Mindful Communication with Others			
	Did What was Effective			
	Completed a Task Mindfully			
Emotion Regulation	Engaged in Physical Regulation of Mood			
	Balanced Thoughts and Feelings			
	Experienced Positive Events			
	Let Go of Thoughts or Judgments			
	Watched and Named Emotions			
	Didn't Act on Emotions			
	Used Opposite Action			
	Used Problem Solving			
Interpersonal Effectiveness	Practiced Compassion for Others			
	Made an Assertive Request			
	Said No Assertively			
	Negotiated Agreements			
	Listened to and Understood Others			
	Validated Others			
Exposure-Based Cognitive Rehearsal	Practiced Exposure-Based Cognitive Rehearsal Skill			
Rate Your Overall Mood for the Day (0 to 10)				

Th	F	Sa	S	NOTES

WEEK 2.

Core Skills	Coping Strategies	M	T	W
Distress Tolerance	Stopped Self-Destructive Action			
	Used the REST Strategy			
	Used Radical Acceptance			
	Distracted from Pain			
	Engaged in Pleasurable Activities			
	Soothed Myself			
	Practiced Relaxation			
	Committed to Valued Action			
	Rehearsed Values-Based Behavior			
	Connected with My Higher Power			
	Used Coping Thoughts			
	Determined Feelings-Threat Balance			
	Used Coping Strategies			
	Used Physiological-Coping Skills			
Mindfulness	Practiced Mindful Breathing			
	Used Wise Mind			
	Practiced Beginner's Mind			
	Practiced Self-Compassion			
	Used Mindful Communication with Others			
	Did What was Effective			
	Completed a Task Mindfully			
Emotion Regulation	Engaged in Physical Regulation of Mood			
	Balanced Thoughts and Feelings			
	Experienced Positive Events			
	Let Go of Thoughts or Judgments			
	Watched and Named Emotions			
	Didn't Act on Emotions			
	Used Opposite Action			
	Used Problem Solving			
Interpersonal Effectiveness	Practiced Compassion for Others			
	Made an Assertive Request			
	Said No Assertively			
	Negotiated Agreements			
	Listened to and Understood Others			
	Validated Others			
Exposure-Based Cognitive Rehearsal	Practiced Exposure-Based Cognitive Rehearsal Skill			
Rate Your Overall Mood for the Day (0 to 10)				

Th	F	Sa	S	NOTES

WEEK 3.

Core Skills	Coping Strategies	M	T	W
Distress Tolerance	Stopped Self-Destructive Action			
	Used the REST Strategy			
	Used Radical Acceptance			
	Distracted from Pain			
	Engaged in Pleasurable Activities			
	Soothed Myself			
	Practiced Relaxation			
	Committed to Valued Action			
	Rehearsed Values-Based Behavior			
	Connected with My Higher Power			
	Used Coping Thoughts			
	Determined Feelings-Threat Balance			
	Used Coping Strategies			
	Used Physiological-Coping Skills			
Mindfulness	Practiced Mindful Breathing			
	Used Wise Mind			
	Practiced Beginner's Mind			
	Practiced Self-Compassion			
	Used Mindful Communication with Others			
	Did What was Effective			
	Completed a Task Mindfully			
Emotion Regulation	Engaged in Physical Regulation of Mood			
	Balanced Thoughts and Feelings			
	Experienced Positive Events			
	Let Go of Thoughts or Judgments			
	Watched and Named Emotions			
	Didn't Act on Emotions			
	Used Opposite Action			
	Used Problem Solving			
Interpersonal Effectiveness	Practiced Compassion for Others			
	Made an Assertive Request			
	Said No Assertively			
	Negotiated Agreements			
	Listened to and Understood Others			
	Validated Others			
Exposure-Based Cognitive Rehearsal	Practiced Exposure-Based Cognitive Rehearsal Skill			
Rate Your Overall Mood for the Day (0 to 10)				

71

Th	F	Sa	S	NOTES

WEEK 4.

Core Skills	Coping Strategies	M	T	W
Distress Tolerance	Stopped Self-Destructive Action			
	Used the REST Strategy			
	Used Radical Acceptance			
	Distracted from Pain			
	Engaged in Pleasurable Activities			
	Soothed Myself			
	Practiced Relaxation			
	Committed to Valued Action			
	Rehearsed Values-Based Behavior			
	Connected with My Higher Power			
	Used Coping Thoughts			
	Determined Feelings-Threat Balance			
	Used Coping Strategies			
	Used Physiological-Coping Skills			
Mindfulness	Practiced Mindful Breathing			
	Used Wise Mind			
	Practiced Beginner's Mind			
	Practiced Self-Compassion			
	Used Mindful Communication with Others			
	Did What was Effective			
	Completed a Task Mindfully			
Emotion Regulation	Engaged in Physical Regulation of Mood			
	Balanced Thoughts and Feelings			
	Experienced Positive Events			
	Let Go of Thoughts or Judgments			
	Watched and Named Emotions			
	Didn't Act on Emotions			
	Used Opposite Action			
	Used Problem Solving			
Interpersonal Effectiveness	Practiced Compassion for Others			
	Made an Assertive Request			
	Said No Assertively			
	Negotiated Agreements			
	Listened to and Understood Others			
	Validated Others			
Exposure-Based Cognitive Rehearsal	Practiced Exposure-Based Cognitive Rehearsal Skill			
Rate Your Overall Mood for the Day (0 to 10)				

Th	F	Sa	S	NOTES

WEEK 5.

Core Skills	Coping Strategies	M	T	W
Distress Tolerance	Stopped Self-Destructive Action			
	Used the REST Strategy			
	Used Radical Acceptance			
	Distracted from Pain			
	Engaged in Pleasurable Activities			
	Soothed Myself			
	Practiced Relaxation			
	Committed to Valued Action			
	Rehearsed Values-Based Behavior			
	Connected with My Higher Power			
	Used Coping Thoughts			
	Determined Feelings-Threat Balance			
	Used Coping Strategies			
	Used Physiological-Coping Skills			
Mindfulness	Practiced Mindful Breathing			
	Used Wise Mind			
	Practiced Beginner's Mind			
	Practiced Self-Compassion			
	Used Mindful communication with Others			
	Did What was Effective			
	Completed a Task Mindfully			
Emotion Regulation	Engaged in Physical Regulation of Mood			
	Balanced Thoughts and Feelings			
	Experienced Positive Events			
	Let Go of Thoughts or Judgments			
	Watched and Named Emotions			
	Didn't Act on Emotions			
	Used Opposite Action			
	Used Problem Solving			
Interpersonal Effectiveness	Practiced Compassion for Others			
	Made an Assertive Request			
	Said No Assertively			
	Negotiated Agreements			
	Listened to and Understood Others			
	Validated Others			
Exposure-Based Cognitive Rehearsal	Practiced Exposure-Based Cognitive Rehearsal Skill			
Rate Your Overall Mood for the Day (0 to 10)				

Th	F	Sa	S	NOTES

WEEK 6.

Core Skills	Coping Strategies	M	T	W
Distress Tolerance	Stopped Self-Destructive Action			
	Used the REST Strategy			
	Used Radical Acceptance			
	Distracted from Pain			
	Engaged in Pleasurable Activities			
	Soothed Myself			
	Practiced Relaxation			
	Committed to Valued Action			
	Rehearsed Values-Based Behavior			
	Connected with My Higher Power			
	Used Coping Thoughts			
	Determined Feelings-Threat Balance			
	Used Coping Strategies			
	Used Physiological-Coping Skills			
Mindfulness	Practiced Mindful Breathing			
	Used Wise Mind			
	Practiced Beginner's Mind			
	Practiced Self-Compassion			
	Used Mindful communication with Others			
	Did What was Effective			
	Completed a Task Mindfully			
Emotion Regulation	Engaged in Physical Regulation of Mood			
	Balanced Thoughts and Feelings			
	Experienced Positive Events			
	Let Go of Thoughts or Judgments			
	Watched and Named Emotions			
	Didn't Act on Emotions			
	Used Opposite Action			
	Used Problem Solving			
Interpersonal Effectiveness	Practiced Compassion for Others			
	Made an Assertive Request			
	Said No Assertively			
	Negotiated Agreements			
	Listened to and Understood Others			
	Validated Others			
Exposure-Based Cognitive Rehearsal	Practiced Exposure-Based Cognitive Rehearsal Skill			
Rate Your Overall Mood for the Day (0 to 10)				

Th	F	Sa	S	NOTES

WEEK 7.

Core Skills	Coping Strategies	M	T	W
Distress Tolerance	Stopped Self-Destructive Action			
	Used the REST Strategy			
	Used Radical Acceptance			
	Distracted from Pain			
	Engaged in Pleasurable Activities			
	Soothed Myself			
	Practiced Relaxation			
	Committed to Valued Action			
	Rehearsed Values-Based Behavior			
	Connected with My Higher Power			
	Used Coping Thoughts			
	Determined Feelings-Threat Balance			
	Used Coping Strategies			
	Used Physiological-Coping Skills			
Mindfulness	Practiced Mindful Breathing			
	Used Wise Mind			
	Practiced Beginner's Mind			
	Practiced Self-Compassion			
	Used Mindful communication with Others			
	Did What was Effective			
	Completed a Task Mindfully			
Emotion Regulation	Engaged in Physical Regulation of Mood			
	Balanced Thoughts and Feelings			
	Experienced Positive Events			
	Let Go of Thoughts or Judgments			
	Watched and Named Emotions			
	Didn't Act on Emotions			
	Used Opposite Action			
	Used Problem Solving			
Interpersonal Effectiveness	Practiced Compassion for Others			
	Made an Assertive Request			
	Said No Assertively			
	Negotiated Agreements			
	Listened to and Understood Others			
	Validated Others			
Exposure-Based Cognitive Rehearsal	Practiced Exposure-Based Cognitive Rehearsal Skill			
Rate Your Overall Mood for the Day (0 to 10)				

Th	F	Sa	S	NOTES

WEEK 8.

Core Skills	Coping Strategies	M	T	W
Distress Tolerance	Stopped Self-Destructive Action			
	Used the REST Strategy			
	Used Radical Acceptance			
	Distracted from Pain			
	Engaged in Pleasurable Activities			
	Soothed Myself			
	Practiced Relaxation			
	Committed to Valued Action			
	Rehearsed Values-Based Behavior			
	Connected with My Higher Power			
	Used Coping Thoughts			
	Determined Feelings-Threat Balance			
	Used Coping Strategies			
	Used Physiological-Coping Skills			
Mindfulness	Practiced Mindful Breathing			
	Used Wise Mind			
	Practiced Beginner's Mind			
	Practiced Self-Compassion			
	Used Mindful communication with Others			
	Did What was Effective			
	Completed a Task Mindfully			
Emotion Regulation	Engaged in Physical Regulation of Mood			
	Balanced Thoughts and Feelings			
	Experienced Positive Events			
	Let Go of Thoughts or Judgments			
	Watched and Named Emotions			
	Didn't Act on Emotions			
	Used Opposite Action			
	Used Problem Solving			
Interpersonal Effectiveness	Practiced Compassion for Others			
	Made an Assertive Request			
	Said No Assertively			
	Negotiated Agreements			
	Listened to and Understood Others			
	Validated Others			
Exposure-Based Cognitive Rehearsal	Practiced Exposure-Based Cognitive Rehearsal Skill			
Rate Your Overall Mood for the Day (0 to 10)				

Th	F	Sa	S	NOTES

WEEK 9.

Core Skills	Coping Strategies	M	T	W
Distress Tolerance	Stopped Self-Destructive Action			
	Used the REST Strategy			
	Used Radical Acceptance			
	Distracted from Pain			
	Engaged in Pleasurable Activities			
	Soothed Myself			
	Practiced Relaxation			
	Committed to Valued Action			
	Rehearsed Values-Based Behavior			
	Connected with My Higher Power			
	Used Coping Thoughts			
	Determined Feelings-Threat Balance			
	Used Coping Strategies			
	Used Physiological-Coping Skills			
Mindfulness	Practiced Mindful Breathing			
	Used Wise Mind			
	Practiced Beginner's Mind			
	Practiced Self-Compassion			
	Used Mindful communication with Others			
	Did What was Effective			
	Completed a Task Mindfully			
Emotion Regulation	Engaged in Physical Regulation of Mood			
	Balanced Thoughts and Feelings			
	Experienced Positive Events			
	Let Go of Thoughts or Judgments			
	Watched and Named Emotions			
	Didn't Act on Emotions			
	Used Opposite Action			
	Used Problem Solving			
Interpersonal Effectiveness	Practiced Compassion for Others			
	Made an Assertive Request			
	Said No Assertively			
	Negotiated Agreements			
	Listened to and Understood Others			
	Validated Others			
Exposure-Based Cognitive Rehearsal	Practiced Exposure-Based Cognitive Rehearsal Skill			
Rate Your Overall Mood for the Day (0 to 10)				

Th	F	Sa	S	NOTES

WEEK 10.

Core Skills	Coping Strategies	M	T	W
Distress Tolerance	Stopped Self-Destructive Action			
	Used the REST Strategy			
	Used Radical Acceptance			
	Distracted from Pain			
	Engaged in Pleasurable Activities			
	Soothed Myself			
	Practiced Relaxation			
	Committed to Valued Action			
	Rehearsed Values-Based Behavior			
	Connected with My Higher Power			
	Used Coping Thoughts			
	Determined Feelings-Threat Balance			
	Used Coping Strategies			
	Used Physiological-Coping Skills			
Mindfulness	Practiced Mindful Breathing			
	Used Wise Mind			
	Practiced Beginner's Mind			
	Practiced Self-Compassion			
	Used Mindful communication with Others			
	Did What was Effective			
	Completed a Task Mindfully			
Emotion Regulation	Engaged in Physical Regulation of Mood			
	Balanced Thoughts and Feelings			
	Experienced Positive Events			
	Let Go of Thoughts or Judgments			
	Watched and Named Emotions			
	Didn't Act on Emotions			
	Used Opposite Action			
	Used Problem Solving			
Interpersonal Effectiveness	Practiced Compassion for Others			
	Made an Assertive Request			
	Said No Assertively			
	Negotiated Agreements			
	Listened to and Understood Others			
	Validated Others			
Exposure-Based Cognitive Rehearsal	Practiced Exposure-Based Cognitive Rehearsal Skill			
Rate Your Overall Mood for the Day (0 to 10)				

85

Th	F	Sa	S	NOTES

WEEK 11.

Core Skills	Coping Strategies	M	T	W
Distress Tolerance	Stopped Self-Destructive Action			
	Used the REST Strategy			
	Used Radical Acceptance			
	Distracted from Pain			
	Engaged in Pleasurable Activities			
	Soothed Myself			
	Practiced Relaxation			
	Committed to Valued Action			
	Rehearsed Values-Based Behavior			
	Connected with My Higher Power			
	Used Coping Thoughts			
	Determined Feelings-Threat Balance			
	Used Coping Strategies			
	Used Physiological-Coping Skills			
Mindfulness	Practiced Mindful Breathing			
	Used Wise Mind			
	Practiced Beginner's Mind			
	Practiced Self-Compassion			
	Used Mindful communication with Others			
	Did What was Effective			
	Completed a Task Mindfully			
Emotion Regulation	Engaged in Physical Regulation of Mood			
	Balanced Thoughts and Feelings			
	Experienced Positive Events			
	Let Go of Thoughts or Judgments			
	Watched and Named Emotions			
	Didn't Act on Emotions			
	Used Opposite Action			
	Used Problem Solving			
Interpersonal Effectiveness	Practiced Compassion for Others			
	Made an Assertive Request			
	Said No Assertively			
	Negotiated Agreements			
	Listened to and Understood Others			
	Validated Others			
Exposure-Based Cognitive Rehearsal	Practiced Exposure-Based Cognitive Rehearsal Skill			
Rate Your Overall Mood for the Day (0 to 10)				

Th	F	Sa	S	NOTES

WEEK 12.

Core Skills	Coping Strategies	M	T	W
Distress Tolerance	Stopped Self-Destructive Action			
	Used the REST Strategy			
	Used Radical Acceptance			
	Distracted from Pain			
	Engaged in Pleasurable Activities			
	Soothed Myself			
	Practiced Relaxation			
	Committed to Valued Action			
	Rehearsed Values-Based Behavior			
	Connected with My Higher Power			
	Used Coping Thoughts			
	Determined Feelings-Threat Balance			
	Used Coping Strategies			
	Used Physiological-Coping Skills			
Mindfulness	Practiced Mindful Breathing			
	Used Wise Mind			
	Practiced Beginner's Mind			
	Practiced Self-Compassion			
	Used Mindful communication with Others			
	Did What was Effective			
	Completed a Task Mindfully			
Emotion Regulation	Engaged in Physical Regulation of Mood			
	Balanced Thoughts and Feelings			
	Experienced Positive Events			
	Let Go of Thoughts or Judgments			
	Watched and Named Emotions			
	Didn't Act on Emotions			
	Used Opposite Action			
	Used Problem Solving			
Interpersonal Effectiveness	Practiced Compassion for Others			
	Made an Assertive Request			
	Said No Assertively			
	Negotiated Agreements			
	Listened to and Understood Others			
	Validated Others			
Exposure-Based Cognitive Rehearsal	Practiced Exposure-Based Cognitive Rehearsal Skill			
Rate Your Overall Mood for the Day (0 to 10)				

Th	F	Sa	S	NOTES

WEEK 13.

Core Skills	Coping Strategies	M	T	W
Distress Tolerance	Stopped Self-Destructive Action			
	Used the REST Strategy			
	Used Radical Acceptance			
	Distracted from Pain			
	Engaged in Pleasurable Activities			
	Soothed Myself			
	Practiced Relaxation			
	Committed to Valued Action			
	Rehearsed Values-Based Behavior			
	Connected with My Higher Power			
	Used Coping Thoughts			
	Determined Feelings-Threat Balance			
	Used Coping Strategies			
	Used Physiological-Coping Skills			
Mindfulness	Practiced Mindful Breathing			
	Used Wise Mind			
	Practiced Beginner's Mind			
	Practiced Self-Compassion			
	Used Mindful communication with Others			
	Did What was Effective			
	Completed a Task Mindfully			
Emotion Regulation	Engaged in Physical Regulation of Mood			
	Balanced Thoughts and Feelings			
	Experienced Positive Events			
	Let Go of Thoughts or Judgments			
	Watched and Named Emotions			
	Didn't Act on Emotions			
	Used Opposite Action			
	Used Problem Solving			
Interpersonal Effectiveness	Practiced Compassion for Others			
	Made an Assertive Request			
	Said No Assertively			
	Negotiated Agreements			
	Listened to and Understood Others			
	Validated Others			
Exposure-Based Cognitive Rehearsal	Practiced Exposure-Based Cognitive Rehearsal Skill			
Rate Your Overall Mood for the Day (0 to 10)				

91

Th	F	Sa	S	NOTES

WEEK 14.

Core Skills	Coping Strategies	M	T	W
Distress Tolerance	Stopped Self-Destructive Action			
	Used the REST Strategy			
	Used Radical Acceptance			
	Distracted from Pain			
	Engaged in Pleasurable Activities			
	Soothed Myself			
	Practiced Relaxation			
	Committed to Valued Action			
	Rehearsed Values-Based Behavior			
	Connected with My Higher Power			
	Used Coping Thoughts			
	Determined Feelings-Threat Balance			
	Used Coping Strategies			
	Used Physiological-Coping Skills			
Mindfulness	Practiced Mindful Breathing			
	Used Wise Mind			
	Practiced Beginner's Mind			
	Practiced Self-Compassion			
	Used Mindful communication with Others			
	Did What was Effective			
	Completed a Task Mindfully			
Emotion Regulation	Engaged in Physical Regulation of Mood			
	Balanced Thoughts and Feelings			
	Experienced Positive Events			
	Let Go of Thoughts or Judgments			
	Watched and Named Emotions			
	Didn't Act on Emotions			
	Used Opposite Action			
	Used Problem Solving			
Interpersonal Effectiveness	Practiced Compassion for Others			
	Made an Assertive Request			
	Said No Assertively			
	Negotiated Agreements			
	Listened to and Understood Others			
	Validated Others			
Exposure-Based Cognitive Rehearsal	Practiced Exposure-Based Cognitive Rehearsal Skill			
Rate Your Overall Mood for the Day (0 to 10)				

Th	F	Sa	S	NOTES

WEEK 15.

Core Skills	Coping Strategies	M	T	W
Distress Tolerance	Stopped Self-Destructive Action			
	Used the REST Strategy			
	Used Radical Acceptance			
	Distracted from Pain			
	Engaged in Pleasurable Activities			
	Soothed Myself			
	Practiced Relaxation			
	Committed to Valued Action			
	Rehearsed Values-Based Behavior			
	Connected with My Higher Power			
	Used Coping Thoughts			
	Determined Feelings-Threat Balance			
	Used Coping Strategies			
	Used Physiological-Coping Skills			
Mindfulness	Practiced Mindful Breathing			
	Used Wise Mind			
	Practiced Beginner's Mind			
	Practiced Self-Compassion			
	Used Mindful communication with Others			
	Did What was Effective			
	Completed a Task Mindfully			
Emotion Regulation	Engaged in Physical Regulation of Mood			
	Balanced Thoughts and Feelings			
	Experienced Positive Events			
	Let Go of Thoughts or Judgments			
	Watched and Named Emotions			
	Didn't Act on Emotions			
	Used Opposite Action			
	Used Problem Solving			
Interpersonal Effectiveness	Practiced Compassion for Others			
	Made an Assertive Request			
	Said No Assertively			
	Negotiated Agreements			
	Listened to and Understood Others			
	Validated Others			
Exposure-Based Cognitive Rehearsal	Practiced Exposure-Based Cognitive Rehearsal Skill			
Rate Your Overall Mood for the Day (0 to 10)				

Th	F	Sa	S	NOTES

WEEK 16.

Core Skills	Coping Strategies	M	T	W
Distress Tolerance	Stopped Self-Destructive Action			
	Used the REST Strategy			
	Used Radical Acceptance			
	Distracted from Pain			
	Engaged in Pleasurable Activities			
	Soothed Myself			
	Practiced Relaxation			
	Committed to Valued Action			
	Rehearsed Values-Based Behavior			
	Connected with My Higher Power			
	Used Coping Thoughts			
	Determined Feelings-Threat Balance			
	Used Coping Strategies			
	Used Physiological-Coping Skills			
Mindfulness	Practiced Mindful Breathing			
	Used Wise Mind			
	Practiced Beginner's Mind			
	Practiced Self-Compassion			
	Used Mindful communication with Others			
	Did What was Effective			
	Completed a Task Mindfully			
Emotion Regulation	Engaged in Physical Regulation of Mood			
	Balanced Thoughts and Feelings			
	Experienced Positive Events			
	Let Go of Thoughts or Judgments			
	Watched and Named Emotions			
	Didn't Act on Emotions			
	Used Opposite Action			
	Used Problem Solving			
Interpersonal Effectiveness	Practiced Compassion for Others			
	Made an Assertive Request			
	Said No Assertively			
	Negotiated Agreements			
	Listened to and Understood Others			
	Validated Others			
Exposure-Based Cognitive Rehearsal	Practiced Exposure-Based Cognitive Rehearsal Skill			
Rate Your Overall Mood for the Day (0 to 10)				

Th	F	Sa	S	NOTES

WEEK 17.

Core Skills	Coping Strategies	M	T	W
Distress Tolerance	Stopped Self-Destructive Action			
	Used the REST Strategy			
	Used Radical Acceptance			
	Distracted from Pain			
	Engaged in Pleasurable Activities			
	Soothed Myself			
	Practiced Relaxation			
	Committed to Valued Action			
	Rehearsed Values-Based Behavior			
	Connected with My Higher Power			
	Used Coping Thoughts			
	Determined Feelings-Threat Balance			
	Used Coping Strategies			
	Used Physiological-Coping Skills			
Mindfulness	Practiced Mindful Breathing			
	Used Wise Mind			
	Practiced Beginner's Mind			
	Practiced Self-Compassion			
	Used Mindful communication with Others			
	Did What was Effective			
	Completed a Task Mindfully			
Emotion Regulation	Engaged in Physical Regulation of Mood			
	Balanced Thoughts and Feelings			
	Experienced Positive Events			
	Let Go of Thoughts or Judgments			
	Watched and Named Emotions			
	Didn't Act on Emotions			
	Used Opposite Action			
	Used Problem Solving			
Interpersonal Effectiveness	Practiced Compassion for Others			
	Made an Assertive Request			
	Said No Assertively			
	Negotiated Agreements			
	Listened to and Understood Others			
	Validated Others			
Exposure-Based Cognitive Rehearsal	Practiced Exposure-Based Cognitive Rehearsal Skill			
Rate Your Overall Mood for the Day (0 to 10)				

Th	F	Sa	S	NOTES

WEEK 18.

Core Skills	Coping Strategies	M	T	W
Distress Tolerance	Stopped Self-Destructive Action			
	Used the REST Strategy			
	Used Radical Acceptance			
	Distracted from Pain			
	Engaged in Pleasurable Activities			
	Soothed Myself			
	Practiced Relaxation			
	Committed to Valued Action			
	Rehearsed Values-Based Behavior			
	Connected with My Higher Power			
	Used Coping Thoughts			
	Determined Feelings-Threat Balance			
	Used Coping Strategies			
	Used Physiological-Coping Skills			
Mindfulness	Practiced Mindful Breathing			
	Used Wise Mind			
	Practiced Beginner's Mind			
	Practiced Self-Compassion			
	Used Mindful communication with Others			
	Did What was Effective			
	Completed a Task Mindfully			
Emotion Regulation	Engaged in Physical Regulation of Mood			
	Balanced Thoughts and Feelings			
	Experienced Positive Events			
	Let Go of Thoughts or Judgments			
	Watched and Named Emotions			
	Didn't Act on Emotions			
	Used Opposite Action			
	Used Problem Solving			
Interpersonal Effectiveness	Practiced Compassion for Others			
	Made an Assertive Request			
	Said No Assertively			
	Negotiated Agreements			
	Listened to and Understood Others			
	Validated Others			
Exposure-Based Cognitive Rehearsal	Practiced Exposure-Based Cognitive Rehearsal Skill			
Rate Your Overall Mood for the Day (0 to 10)				

Th	F	Sa	S	NOTES

WEEK 19.

Core Skills	Coping Strategies	M	T	W
Distress Tolerance	Stopped Self-Destructive Action			
	Used the REST Strategy			
	Used Radical Acceptance			
	Distracted from Pain			
	Engaged in Pleasurable Activities			
	Soothed Myself			
	Practiced Relaxation			
	Committed to Valued Action			
	Rehearsed Values-Based Behavior			
	Connected with My Higher Power			
	Used Coping Thoughts			
	Determined Feelings-Threat Balance			
	Used Coping Strategies			
	Used Physiological-Coping Skills			
Mindfulness	Practiced Mindful Breathing			
	Used Wise Mind			
	Practiced Beginner's Mind			
	Practiced Self-Compassion			
	Used Mindful communication with Others			
	Did What was Effective			
	Completed a Task Mindfully			
Emotion Regulation	Engaged in Physical Regulation of Mood			
	Balanced Thoughts and Feelings			
	Experienced Positive Events			
	Let Go of Thoughts or Judgments			
	Watched and Named Emotions			
	Didn't Act on Emotions			
	Used Opposite Action			
	Used Problem Solving			
Interpersonal Effectiveness	Practiced Compassion for Others			
	Made an Assertive Request			
	Said No Assertively			
	Negotiated Agreements			
	Listened to and Understood Others			
	Validated Others			
Exposure-Based Cognitive Rehearsal	Practiced Exposure-Based Cognitive Rehearsal Skill			
Rate Your Overall Mood for the Day (0 to 10)				

Th	F	Sa	S	NOTES

Core Skills	Coping Strategies	M	T	W
Distress Tolerance	Stopped Self-Destructive Action			
	Used the REST Strategy			
	Used Radical Acceptance			
	Distracted from Pain			
	Engaged in Pleasurable Activities			
	Soothed Myself			
	Practiced Relaxation			
	Committed to Valued Action			
	Rehearsed Values-Based Behavior			
	Connected with My Higher Power			
	Used Coping Thoughts			
	Determined Feelings-Threat Balance			
	Used Coping Strategies			
	Used Physiological-Coping Skills			
Mindfulness	Practiced Mindful Breathing			
	Used Wise Mind			
	Practiced Beginner's Mind			
	Practiced Self-Compassion			
	Used Mindful communication with Others			
	Did What was Effective			
	Completed a Task Mindfully			
Emotion Regulation	Engaged in Physical Regulation of Mood			
	Balanced Thoughts and Feelings			
	Experienced Positive Events			
	Let Go of Thoughts or Judgments			
	Watched and Named Emotions			
	Didn't Act on Emotions			
	Used Opposite Action			
	Used Problem Solving			
Interpersonal Effectiveness	Practiced Compassion for Others			
	Made an Assertive Request			
	Said No Assertively			
	Negotiated Agreements			
	Listened to and Understood Others			
	Validated Others			
Exposure-Based Cognitive Rehearsal	Practiced Exposure-Based Cognitive Rehearsal Skill			
Rate Your Overall Mood for the Day (0 to 10)				

105

Th	F	Sa	S	NOTES

WEEK 21.

Core Skills	Coping Strategies	M	T	W
Distress Tolerance	Stopped Self-Destructive Action			
	Used the REST Strategy			
	Used Radical Acceptance			
	Distracted from Pain			
	Engaged in Pleasurable Activities			
	Soothed Myself			
	Practiced Relaxation			
	Committed to Valued Action			
	Rehearsed Values-Based Behavior			
	Connected with My Higher Power			
	Used Coping Thoughts			
	Determined Feelings-Threat Balance			
	Used Coping Strategies			
	Used Physiological-Coping Skills			
Mindfulness	Practiced Mindful Breathing			
	Used Wise Mind			
	Practiced Beginner's Mind			
	Practiced Self-Compassion			
	Used Mindful communication with Others			
	Did What was Effective			
	Completed a Task Mindfully			
Emotion Regulation	Engaged in Physical Regulation of Mood			
	Balanced Thoughts and Feelings			
	Experienced Positive Events			
	Let Go of Thoughts or Judgments			
	Watched and Named Emotions			
	Didn't Act on Emotions			
	Used Opposite Action			
	Used Problem Solving			
Interpersonal Effectiveness	Practiced Compassion for Others			
	Made an Assertive Request			
	Said No Assertively			
	Negotiated Agreements			
	Listened to and Understood Others			
	Validated Others			
Exposure-Based Cognitive Rehearsal	Practiced Exposure-Based Cognitive Rehearsal Skill			
Rate Your Overall Mood for the Day (0 to 10)				

Th	F	Sa	S	NOTES

WEEK 22.

Core Skills	Coping Strategies	M	T	W
Distress Tolerance	Stopped Self-Destructive Action			
	Used the REST Strategy			
	Used Radical Acceptance			
	Distracted from Pain			
	Engaged in Pleasurable Activities			
	Soothed Myself			
	Practiced Relaxation			
	Committed to Valued Action			
	Rehearsed Values-Based Behavior			
	Connected with My Higher Power			
	Used Coping Thoughts			
	Determined Feelings-Threat Balance			
	Used Coping Strategies			
	Used Physiological-Coping Skills			
Mindfulness	Practiced Mindful Breathing			
	Used Wise Mind			
	Practiced Beginner's Mind			
	Practiced Self-Compassion			
	Used Mindful communication with Others			
	Did What was Effective			
	Completed a Task Mindfully			
Emotion Regulation	Engaged in Physical Regulation of Mood			
	Balanced Thoughts and Feelings			
	Experienced Positive Events			
	Let Go of Thoughts or Judgments			
	Watched and Named Emotions			
	Didn't Act on Emotions			
	Used Opposite Action			
	Used Problem Solving			
Interpersonal Effectiveness	Practiced Compassion for Others			
	Made an Assertive Request			
	Said No Assertively			
	Negotiated Agreements			
	Listened to and Understood Others			
	Validated Others			
Exposure-Based Cognitive Rehearsal	Practiced Exposure-Based Cognitive Rehearsal Skill			
Rate Your Overall Mood for the Day (0 to 10)				

109

Th	F	Sa	S	NOTES

WEEK 23.

Core Skills	Coping Strategies	M	T	W
Distress Tolerance	Stopped Self-Destructive Action			
	Used the REST Strategy			
	Used Radical Acceptance			
	Distracted from Pain			
	Engaged in Pleasurable Activities			
	Soothed Myself			
	Practiced Relaxation			
	Committed to Valued Action			
	Rehearsed Values-Based Behavior			
	Connected with My Higher Power			
	Used Coping Thoughts			
	Determined Feelings-Threat Balance			
	Used Coping Strategies			
	Used Physiological-Coping Skills			
Mindfulness	Practiced Mindful Breathing			
	Used Wise Mind			
	Practiced Beginner's Mind			
	Practiced Self-Compassion			
	Used Mindful communication with Others			
	Did What was Effective			
	Completed a Task Mindfully			
Emotion Regulation	Engaged in Physical Regulation of Mood			
	Balanced Thoughts and Feelings			
	Experienced Positive Events			
	Let Go of Thoughts or Judgments			
	Watched and Named Emotions			
	Didn't Act on Emotions			
	Used Opposite Action			
	Used Problem Solving			
Interpersonal Effectiveness	Practiced Compassion for Others			
	Made an Assertive Request			
	Said No Assertively			
	Negotiated Agreements			
	Listened to and Understood Others			
	Validated Others			
Exposure-Based Cognitive Rehearsal	Practiced Exposure-Based Cognitive Rehearsal Skill			
Rate Your Overall Mood for the Day (0 to 10)				

Th	F	Sa	S	NOTES

WEEK 24.

Core Skills	Coping Strategies	M	T	W
Distress Tolerance	Stopped Self-Destructive Action			
	Used the REST Strategy			
	Used Radical Acceptance			
	Distracted from Pain			
	Engaged in Pleasurable Activities			
	Soothed Myself			
	Practiced Relaxation			
	Committed to Valued Action			
	Rehearsed Values-Based Behavior			
	Connected with My Higher Power			
	Used Coping Thoughts			
	Determined Feelings-Threat Balance			
	Used Coping Strategies			
	Used Physiological-Coping Skills			
Mindfulness	Practiced Mindful Breathing			
	Used Wise Mind			
	Practiced Beginner's Mind			
	Practiced Self-Compassion			
	Used Mindful communication with Others			
	Did What was Effective			
	Completed a Task Mindfully			
Emotion Regulation	Engaged in Physical Regulation of Mood			
	Balanced Thoughts and Feelings			
	Experienced Positive Events			
	Let Go of Thoughts or Judgments			
	Watched and Named Emotions			
	Didn't Act on Emotions			
	Used Opposite Action			
	Used Problem Solving			
Interpersonal Effectiveness	Practiced Compassion for Others			
	Made an Assertive Request			
	Said No Assertively			
	Negotiated Agreements			
	Listened to and Understood Others			
	Validated Others			
Exposure-Based Cognitive Rehearsal	Practiced Exposure-Based Cognitive Rehearsal Skill			
Rate Your Overall Mood for the Day (0 to 10)				

Th	F	Sa	S	NOTES

WEEK 25.

Core Skills	Coping Strategies	M	T	W
Distress Tolerance	Stopped Self-Destructive Action			
	Used the REST Strategy			
	Used Radical Acceptance			
	Distracted from Pain			
	Engaged in Pleasurable Activities			
	Soothed Myself			
	Practiced Relaxation			
	Committed to Valued Action			
	Rehearsed Values-Based Behavior			
	Connected with My Higher Power			
	Used Coping Thoughts			
	Determined Feelings-Threat Balance			
	Used Coping Strategies			
	Used Physiological-Coping Skills			
Mindfulness	Practiced Mindful Breathing			
	Used Wise Mind			
	Practiced Beginner's Mind			
	Practiced Self-Compassion			
	Used Mindful communication with Others			
	Did What was Effective			
	Completed a Task Mindfully			
Emotion Regulation	Engaged in Physical Regulation of Mood			
	Balanced Thoughts and Feelings			
	Experienced Positive Events			
	Let Go of Thoughts or Judgments			
	Watched and Named Emotions			
	Didn't Act on Emotions			
	Used Opposite Action			
	Used Problem Solving			
Interpersonal Effectiveness	Practiced Compassion for Others			
	Made an Assertive Request			
	Said No Assertively			
	Negotiated Agreements			
	Listened to and Understood Others			
	Validated Others			
Exposure-Based Cognitive Rehearsal	Practiced Exposure-Based Cognitive Rehearsal Skill			
Rate Your Overall Mood for the Day (0 to 10)				

Th	F	Sa	S	NOTES

WEEK 26.

Core Skills	Coping Strategies	M	T	W
Distress Tolerance	Stopped Self-Destructive Action			
	Used the REST Strategy			
	Used Radical Acceptance			
	Distracted from Pain			
	Engaged in Pleasurable Activities			
	Soothed Myself			
	Practiced Relaxation			
	Committed to Valued Action			
	Rehearsed Values-Based Behavior			
	Connected with My Higher Power			
	Used Coping Thoughts			
	Determined Feelings-Threat Balance			
	Used Coping Strategies			
	Used Physiological-Coping Skills			
Mindfulness	Practiced Mindful Breathing			
	Used Wise Mind			
	Practiced Beginner's Mind			
	Practiced Self-Compassion			
	Used Mindful communication with Others			
	Did What was Effective			
	Completed a Task Mindfully			
Emotion Regulation	Engaged in Physical Regulation of Mood			
	Balanced Thoughts and Feelings			
	Experienced Positive Events			
	Let Go of Thoughts or Judgments			
	Watched and Named Emotions			
	Didn't Act on Emotions			
	Used Opposite Action			
	Used Problem Solving			
Interpersonal Effectiveness	Practiced Compassion for Others			
	Made an Assertive Request			
	Said No Assertively			
	Negotiated Agreements			
	Listened to and Understood Others			
	Validated Others			
Exposure-Based Cognitive Rehearsal	Practiced Exposure-Based Cognitive Rehearsal Skill			
Rate Your Overall Mood for the Day (0 to 10)				

Th	F	Sa	S	NOTES

WEEK 27.

Core Skills	Coping Strategies	M	T	W
Distress Tolerance	Stopped Self-Destructive Action			
	Used the REST Strategy			
	Used Radical Acceptance			
	Distracted from Pain			
	Engaged in Pleasurable Activities			
	Soothed Myself			
	Practiced Relaxation			
	Committed to Valued Action			
	Rehearsed Values-Based Behavior			
	Connected with My Higher Power			
	Used Coping Thoughts			
	Determined Feelings-Threat Balance			
	Used Coping Strategies			
	Used Physiological-Coping Skills			
Mindfulness	Practiced Mindful Breathing			
	Used Wise Mind			
	Practiced Beginner's Mind			
	Practiced Self-Compassion			
	Used Mindful communication with Others			
	Did What was Effective			
	Completed a Task Mindfully			
Emotion Regulation	Engaged in Physical Regulation of Mood			
	Balanced Thoughts and Feelings			
	Experienced Positive Events			
	Let Go of Thoughts or Judgments			
	Watched and Named Emotions			
	Didn't Act on Emotions			
	Used Opposite Action			
	Used Problem Solving			
Interpersonal Effectiveness	Practiced Compassion for Others			
	Made an Assertive Request			
	Said No Assertively			
	Negotiated Agreements			
	Listened to and Understood Others			
	Validated Others			
Exposure-Based Cognitive Rehearsal	Practiced Exposure-Based Cognitive Rehearsal Skill			
Rate Your Overall Mood for the Day (0 to 10)				

Th	F	Sa	S	NOTES

WEEK 28.

Core Skills	Coping Strategies	M	T	W
Distress Tolerance	Stopped Self-Destructive Action			
	Used the REST Strategy			
	Used Radical Acceptance			
	Distracted from Pain			
	Engaged in Pleasurable Activities			
	Soothed Myself			
	Practiced Relaxation			
	Committed to Valued Action			
	Rehearsed Values-Based Behavior			
	Connected with My Higher Power			
	Used Coping Thoughts			
	Determined Feelings-Threat Balance			
	Used Coping Strategies			
	Used Physiological-Coping Skills			
Mindfulness	Practiced Mindful Breathing			
	Used Wise Mind			
	Practiced Beginner's Mind			
	Practiced Self-Compassion			
	Used Mindful communication with Others			
	Did What was Effective			
	Completed a Task Mindfully			
Emotion Regulation	Engaged in Physical Regulation of Mood			
	Balanced Thoughts and Feelings			
	Experienced Positive Events			
	Let Go of Thoughts or Judgments			
	Watched and Named Emotions			
	Didn't Act on Emotions			
	Used Opposite Action			
	Used Problem Solving			
Interpersonal Effectiveness	Practiced Compassion for Others			
	Made an Assertive Request			
	Said No Assertively			
	Negotiated Agreements			
	Listened to and Understood Others			
	Validated Others			
Exposure-Based Cognitive Rehearsal	Practiced Exposure-Based Cognitive Rehearsal Skill			
Rate Your Overall Mood for the Day (0 to 10)				

Th	F	Sa	S	NOTES

WEEK 29.

Core Skills	Coping Strategies	M	T	W
Distress Tolerance	Stopped Self-Destructive Action			
	Used the REST Strategy			
	Used Radical Acceptance			
	Distracted from Pain			
	Engaged in Pleasurable Activities			
	Soothed Myself			
	Practiced Relaxation			
	Committed to Valued Action			
	Rehearsed Values-Based Behavior			
	Connected with My Higher Power			
	Used Coping Thoughts			
	Determined Feelings-Threat Balance			
	Used Coping Strategies			
	Used Physiological-Coping Skills			
Mindfulness	Practiced Mindful Breathing			
	Used Wise Mind			
	Practiced Beginner's Mind			
	Practiced Self-Compassion			
	Used Mindful communication with Others			
	Did What was Effective			
	Completed a Task Mindfully			
Emotion Regulation	Engaged in Physical Regulation of Mood			
	Balanced Thoughts and Feelings			
	Experienced Positive Events			
	Let Go of Thoughts or Judgments			
	Watched and Named Emotions			
	Didn't Act on Emotions			
	Used Opposite Action			
	Used Problem Solving			
Interpersonal Effectiveness	Practiced Compassion for Others			
	Made an Assertive Request			
	Said No Assertively			
	Negotiated Agreements			
	Listened to and Understood Others			
	Validated Others			
Exposure-Based Cognitive Rehearsal	Practiced Exposure-Based Cognitive Rehearsal Skill			
Rate Your Overall Mood for the Day (0 to 10)				

Th	F	Sa	S	NOTES

WEEK 30.

Core Skills	Coping Strategies	M	T	W
Distress Tolerance	Stopped Self-Destructive Action			
	Used the REST Strategy			
	Used Radical Acceptance			
	Distracted from Pain			
	Engaged in Pleasurable Activities			
	Soothed Myself			
	Practiced Relaxation			
	Committed to Valued Action			
	Rehearsed Values-Based Behavior			
	Connected with My Higher Power			
	Used Coping Thoughts			
	Determined Feelings-Threat Balance			
	Used Coping Strategies			
	Used Physiological-Coping Skills			
Mindfulness	Practiced Mindful Breathing			
	Used Wise Mind			
	Practiced Beginner's Mind			
	Practiced Self-Compassion			
	Used Mindful communication with Others			
	Did What was Effective			
	Completed a Task Mindfully			
Emotion Regulation	Engaged in Physical Regulation of Mood			
	Balanced Thoughts and Feelings			
	Experienced Positive Events			
	Let Go of Thoughts or Judgments			
	Watched and Named Emotions			
	Didn't Act on Emotions			
	Used Opposite Action			
	Used Problem Solving			
Interpersonal Effectiveness	Practiced Compassion for Others			
	Made an Assertive Request			
	Said No Assertively			
	Negotiated Agreements			
	Listened to and Understood Others			
	Validated Others			
Exposure-Based Cognitive Rehearsal	Practiced Exposure-Based Cognitive Rehearsal Skill			
Rate Your Overall Mood for the Day (0 to 10)				

125

Th	F	Sa	S	NOTES

WEEK 31.

Core Skills	Coping Strategies	M	T	W
Distress Tolerance	Stopped Self-Destructive Action			
	Used the REST Strategy			
	Used Radical Acceptance			
	Distracted from Pain			
	Engaged in Pleasurable Activities			
	Soothed Myself			
	Practiced Relaxation			
	Committed to Valued Action			
	Rehearsed Values-Based Behavior			
	Connected with My Higher Power			
	Used Coping Thoughts			
	Determined Feelings-Threat Balance			
	Used Coping Strategies			
	Used Physiological-Coping Skills			
Mindfulness	Practiced Mindful Breathing			
	Used Wise Mind			
	Practiced Beginner's Mind			
	Practiced Self-Compassion			
	Used Mindful communication with Others			
	Did What was Effective			
	Completed a Task Mindfully			
Emotion Regulation	Engaged in Physical Regulation of Mood			
	Balanced Thoughts and Feelings			
	Experienced Positive Events			
	Let Go of Thoughts or Judgments			
	Watched and Named Emotions			
	Didn't Act on Emotions			
	Used Opposite Action			
	Used Problem Solving			
Interpersonal Effectiveness	Practiced Compassion for Others			
	Made an Assertive Request			
	Said No Assertively			
	Negotiated Agreements			
	Listened to and Understood Others			
	Validated Others			
Exposure-Based Cognitive Rehearsal	Practiced Exposure-Based Cognitive Rehearsal Skill			
Rate Your Overall Mood for the Day (0 to 10)				

Th	F	Sa	S	NOTES

WEEK 32.

Core Skills	Coping Strategies	M	T	W
Distress Tolerance	Stopped Self-Destructive Action			
	Used the REST Strategy			
	Used Radical Acceptance			
	Distracted from Pain			
	Engaged in Pleasurable Activities			
	Soothed Myself			
	Practiced Relaxation			
	Committed to Valued Action			
	Rehearsed Values-Based Behavior			
	Connected with My Higher Power			
	Used Coping Thoughts			
	Determined Feelings-Threat Balance			
	Used Coping Strategies			
	Used Physiological-Coping Skills			
Mindfulness	Practiced Mindful Breathing			
	Used Wise Mind			
	Practiced Beginner's Mind			
	Practiced Self-Compassion			
	Used Mindful communication with Others			
	Did What was Effective			
	Completed a Task Mindfully			
Emotion Regulation	Engaged in Physical Regulation of Mood			
	Balanced Thoughts and Feelings			
	Experienced Positive Events			
	Let Go of Thoughts or Judgments			
	Watched and Named Emotions			
	Didn't Act on Emotions			
	Used Opposite Action			
	Used Problem Solving			
Interpersonal Effectiveness	Practiced Compassion for Others			
	Made an Assertive Request			
	Said No Assertively			
	Negotiated Agreements			
	Listened to and Understood Others			
	Validated Others			
Exposure-Based Cognitive Rehearsal	Practiced Exposure-Based Cognitive Rehearsal Skill			
Rate Your Overall Mood for the Day (0 to 10)				

Th	F	Sa	S	NOTES

Core Skills	Coping Strategies	M	T	W
Distress Tolerance	Stopped Self-Destructive Action			
	Used the REST Strategy			
	Used Radical Acceptance			
	Distracted from Pain			
	Engaged in Pleasurable Activities			
	Soothed Myself			
	Practiced Relaxation			
	Committed to Valued Action			
	Rehearsed Values-Based Behavior			
	Connected with My Higher Power			
	Used Coping Thoughts			
	Determined Feelings-Threat Balance			
	Used Coping Strategies			
	Used Physiological-Coping Skills			
Mindfulness	Practiced Mindful Breathing			
	Used Wise Mind			
	Practiced Beginner's Mind			
	Practiced Self-Compassion			
	Used Mindful communication with Others			
	Did What was Effective			
	Completed a Task Mindfully			
Emotion Regulation	Engaged in Physical Regulation of Mood			
	Balanced Thoughts and Feelings			
	Experienced Positive Events			
	Let Go of Thoughts or Judgments			
	Watched and Named Emotions			
	Didn't Act on Emotions			
	Used Opposite Action			
	Used Problem Solving			
Interpersonal Effectiveness	Practiced Compassion for Others			
	Made an Assertive Request			
	Said No Assertively			
	Negotiated Agreements			
	Listened to and Understood Others			
	Validated Others			
Exposure-Based Cognitive Rehearsal	Practiced Exposure-Based Cognitive Rehearsal Skill			
Rate Your Overall Mood for the Day (0 to 10)				

131

Th	F	Sa	S	NOTES

WEEK 34.

Core Skills	Coping Strategies	M	T	W
Distress Tolerance	Stopped Self-Destructive Action			
	Used the REST Strategy			
	Used Radical Acceptance			
	Distracted from Pain			
	Engaged in Pleasurable Activities			
	Soothed Myself			
	Practiced Relaxation			
	Committed to Valued Action			
	Rehearsed Values-Based Behavior			
	Connected with My Higher Power			
	Used Coping Thoughts			
	Determined Feelings-Threat Balance			
	Used Coping Strategies			
	Used Physiological-Coping Skills			
Mindfulness	Practiced Mindful Breathing			
	Used Wise Mind			
	Practiced Beginner's Mind			
	Practiced Self-Compassion			
	Used Mindful communication with Others			
	Did What was Effective			
	Completed a Task Mindfully			
Emotion Regulation	Engaged in Physical Regulation of Mood			
	Balanced Thoughts and Feelings			
	Experienced Positive Events			
	Let Go of Thoughts or Judgments			
	Watched and Named Emotions			
	Didn't Act on Emotions			
	Used Opposite Action			
	Used Problem Solving			
Interpersonal Effectiveness	Practiced Compassion for Others			
	Made an Assertive Request			
	Said No Assertively			
	Negotiated Agreements			
	Listened to and Understood Others			
	Validated Others			
Exposure-Based Cognitive Rehearsal	Practiced Exposure-Based Cognitive Rehearsal Skill			
Rate Your Overall Mood for the Day (0 to 10)				

Th	F	Sa	S	NOTES

Core Skills	Coping Strategies	M	T	W
Distress Tolerance	Stopped Self-Destructive Action			
	Used the REST Strategy			
	Used Radical Acceptance			
	Distracted from Pain			
	Engaged in Pleasurable Activities			
	Soothed Myself			
	Practiced Relaxation			
	Committed to Valued Action			
	Rehearsed Values-Based Behavior			
	Connected with My Higher Power			
	Used Coping Thoughts			
	Determined Feelings-Threat Balance			
	Used Coping Strategies			
	Used Physiological-Coping Skills			
Mindfulness	Practiced Mindful Breathing			
	Used Wise Mind			
	Practiced Beginner's Mind			
	Practiced Self-Compassion			
	Used Mindful communication with Others			
	Did What was Effective			
	Completed a Task Mindfully			
Emotion Regulation	Engaged in Physical Regulation of Mood			
	Balanced Thoughts and Feelings			
	Experienced Positive Events			
	Let Go of Thoughts or Judgments			
	Watched and Named Emotions			
	Didn't Act on Emotions			
	Used Opposite Action			
	Used Problem Solving			
Interpersonal Effectiveness	Practiced Compassion for Others			
	Made an Assertive Request			
	Said No Assertively			
	Negotiated Agreements			
	Listened to and Understood Others			
	Validated Others			
Exposure-Based Cognitive Rehearsal	Practiced Exposure-Based Cognitive Rehearsal Skill			
Rate Your Overall Mood for the Day (0 to 10)				

Th	F	Sa	S	NOTES

WEEK 36.

Core Skills	Coping Strategies	M	T	W
Distress Tolerance	Stopped Self-Destructive Action			
	Used the REST Strategy			
	Used Radical Acceptance			
	Distracted from Pain			
	Engaged in Pleasurable Activities			
	Soothed Myself			
	Practiced Relaxation			
	Committed to Valued Action			
	Rehearsed Values-Based Behavior			
	Connected with My Higher Power			
	Used Coping Thoughts			
	Determined Feelings-Threat Balance			
	Used Coping Strategies			
	Used Physiological-Coping Skills			
Mindfulness	Practiced Mindful Breathing			
	Used Wise Mind			
	Practiced Beginner's Mind			
	Practiced Self-Compassion			
	Used Mindful communication with Others			
	Did What was Effective			
	Completed a Task Mindfully			
Emotion Regulation	Engaged in Physical Regulation of Mood			
	Balanced Thoughts and Feelings			
	Experienced Positive Events			
	Let Go of Thoughts or Judgments			
	Watched and Named Emotions			
	Didn't Act on Emotions			
	Used Opposite Action			
	Used Problem Solving			
Interpersonal Effectiveness	Practiced Compassion for Others			
	Made an Assertive Request			
	Said No Assertively			
	Negotiated Agreements			
	Listened to and Understood Others			
	Validated Others			
Exposure-Based Cognitive Rehearsal	Practiced Exposure-Based Cognitive Rehearsal Skill			
Rate Your Overall Mood for the Day (0 to 10)				

Th	F	Sa	S	NOTES

WEEK 37.

Core Skills	Coping Strategies	M	T	W
Distress Tolerance	Stopped Self-Destructive Action			
	Used the REST Strategy			
	Used Radical Acceptance			
	Distracted from Pain			
	Engaged in Pleasurable Activities			
	Soothed Myself			
	Practiced Relaxation			
	Committed to Valued Action			
	Rehearsed Values-Based Behavior			
	Connected with My Higher Power			
	Used Coping Thoughts			
	Determined Feelings-Threat Balance			
	Used Coping Strategies			
	Used Physiological-Coping Skills			
Mindfulness	Practiced Mindful Breathing			
	Used Wise Mind			
	Practiced Beginner's Mind			
	Practiced Self-Compassion			
	Used Mindful communication with Others			
	Did What was Effective			
	Completed a Task Mindfully			
Emotion Regulation	Engaged in Physical Regulation of Mood			
	Balanced Thoughts and Feelings			
	Experienced Positive Events			
	Let Go of Thoughts or Judgments			
	Watched and Named Emotions			
	Didn't Act on Emotions			
	Used Opposite Action			
	Used Problem Solving			
Interpersonal Effectiveness	Practiced Compassion for Others			
	Made an Assertive Request			
	Said No Assertively			
	Negotiated Agreements			
	Listened to and Understood Others			
	Validated Others			
Exposure-Based Cognitive Rehearsal	Practiced Exposure-Based Cognitive Rehearsal Skill			
Rate Your Overall Mood for the Day (0 to 10)				

Th	F	Sa	S	NOTES

WEEK 38.

Core Skills	Coping Strategies	M	T	W
Distress Tolerance	Stopped Self-Destructive Action			
	Used the REST Strategy			
	Used Radical Acceptance			
	Distracted from Pain			
	Engaged in Pleasurable Activities			
	Soothed Myself			
	Practiced Relaxation			
	Committed to Valued Action			
	Rehearsed Values-Based Behavior			
	Connected with My Higher Power			
	Used Coping Thoughts			
	Determined Feelings-Threat Balance			
	Used Coping Strategies			
	Used Physiological-Coping Skills			
Mindfulness	Practiced Mindful Breathing			
	Used Wise Mind			
	Practiced Beginner's Mind			
	Practiced Self-Compassion			
	Used Mindful communication with Others			
	Did What was Effective			
	Completed a Task Mindfully			
Emotion Regulation	Engaged in Physical Regulation of Mood			
	Balanced Thoughts and Feelings			
	Experienced Positive Events			
	Let Go of Thoughts or Judgments			
	Watched and Named Emotions			
	Didn't Act on Emotions			
	Used Opposite Action			
	Used Problem Solving			
Interpersonal Effectiveness	Practiced Compassion for Others			
	Made an Assertive Request			
	Said No Assertively			
	Negotiated Agreements			
	Listened to and Understood Others			
	Validated Others			
Exposure-Based Cognitive Rehearsal	Practiced Exposure-Based Cognitive Rehearsal Skill			
Rate Your Overall Mood for the Day (0 to 10)				

Th	F	Sa	S	NOTES

WEEK 39.

Core Skills	Coping Strategies	M	T	W
Distress Tolerance	Stopped Self-Destructive Action			
	Used the REST Strategy			
	Used Radical Acceptance			
	Distracted from Pain			
	Engaged in Pleasurable Activities			
	Soothed Myself			
	Practiced Relaxation			
	Committed to Valued Action			
	Rehearsed Values-Based Behavior			
	Connected with My Higher Power			
	Used Coping Thoughts			
	Determined Feelings-Threat Balance			
	Used Coping Strategies			
	Used Physiological-Coping Skills			
Mindfulness	Practiced Mindful Breathing			
	Used Wise Mind			
	Practiced Beginner's Mind			
	Practiced Self-Compassion			
	Used Mindful communication with Others			
	Did What was Effective			
	Completed a Task Mindfully			
Emotion Regulation	Engaged in Physical Regulation of Mood			
	Balanced Thoughts and Feelings			
	Experienced Positive Events			
	Let Go of Thoughts or Judgments			
	Watched and Named Emotions			
	Didn't Act on Emotions			
	Used Opposite Action			
	Used Problem Solving			
Interpersonal Effectiveness	Practiced Compassion for Others			
	Made an Assertive Request			
	Said No Assertively			
	Negotiated Agreements			
	Listened to and Understood Others			
	Validated Others			
Exposure-Based Cognitive Rehearsal	Practiced Exposure-Based Cognitive Rehearsal Skill			
Rate Your Overall Mood for the Day (0 to 10)				

Th	F	Sa	S	NOTES

WEEK 40.

Core Skills	Coping Strategies	M	T	W
Distress Tolerance	Stopped Self-Destructive Action			
	Used the REST Strategy			
	Used Radical Acceptance			
	Distracted from Pain			
	Engaged in Pleasurable Activities			
	Soothed Myself			
	Practiced Relaxation			
	Committed to Valued Action			
	Rehearsed Values-Based Behavior			
	Connected with My Higher Power			
	Used Coping Thoughts			
	Determined Feelings-Threat Balance			
	Used Coping Strategies			
	Used Physiological-Coping Skills			
Mindfulness	Practiced Mindful Breathing			
	Used Wise Mind			
	Practiced Beginner's Mind			
	Practiced Self-Compassion			
	Used Mindful communication with Others			
	Did What was Effective			
	Completed a Task Mindfully			
Emotion Regulation	Engaged in Physical Regulation of Mood			
	Balanced Thoughts and Feelings			
	Experienced Positive Events			
	Let Go of Thoughts or Judgments			
	Watched and Named Emotions			
	Didn't Act on Emotions			
	Used Opposite Action			
	Used Problem Solving			
Interpersonal Effectiveness	Practiced Compassion for Others			
	Made an Assertive Request			
	Said No Assertively			
	Negotiated Agreements			
	Listened to and Understood Others			
	Validated Others			
Exposure-Based Cognitive Rehearsal	Practiced Exposure-Based Cognitive Rehearsal Skill			
Rate Your Overall Mood for the Day (0 to 10)				

Th	F	Sa	S	NOTES

WEEK 41.

Core Skills	Coping Strategies	M	T	W
Distress Tolerance	Stopped Self-Destructive Action			
	Used the REST Strategy			
	Used Radical Acceptance			
	Distracted from Pain			
	Engaged in Pleasurable Activities			
	Soothed Myself			
	Practiced Relaxation			
	Committed to Valued Action			
	Rehearsed Values-Based Behavior			
	Connected with My Higher Power			
	Used Coping Thoughts			
	Determined Feelings-Threat Balance			
	Used Coping Strategies			
	Used Physiological-Coping Skills			
Mindfulness	Practiced Mindful Breathing			
	Used Wise Mind			
	Practiced Beginner's Mind			
	Practiced Self-Compassion			
	Used Mindful communication with Others			
	Did What was Effective			
	Completed a Task Mindfully			
Emotion Regulation	Engaged in Physical Regulation of Mood			
	Balanced Thoughts and Feelings			
	Experienced Positive Events			
	Let Go of Thoughts or Judgments			
	Watched and Named Emotions			
	Didn't Act on Emotions			
	Used Opposite Action			
	Used Problem Solving			
Interpersonal Effectiveness	Practiced Compassion for Others			
	Made an Assertive Request			
	Said No Assertively			
	Negotiated Agreements			
	Listened to and Understood Others			
	Validated Others			
Exposure-Based Cognitive Rehearsal	Practiced Exposure-Based Cognitive Rehearsal Skill			
Rate Your Overall Mood for the Day (0 to 10)				

Th	F	Sa	S	NOTES

WEEK 42.

Core Skills	Coping Strategies	M	T	W
Distress Tolerance	Stopped Self-Destructive Action			
	Used the REST Strategy			
	Used Radical Acceptance			
	Distracted from Pain			
	Engaged in Pleasurable Activities			
	Soothed Myself			
	Practiced Relaxation			
	Committed to Valued Action			
	Rehearsed Values-Based Behavior			
	Connected with My Higher Power			
	Used Coping Thoughts			
	Determined Feelings-Threat Balance			
	Used Coping Strategies			
	Used Physiological-Coping Skills			
Mindfulness	Practiced Mindful Breathing			
	Used Wise Mind			
	Practiced Beginner's Mind			
	Practiced Self-Compassion			
	Used Mindful communication with Others			
	Did What was Effective			
	Completed a Task Mindfully			
Emotion Regulation	Engaged in Physical Regulation of Mood			
	Balanced Thoughts and Feelings			
	Experienced Positive Events			
	Let Go of Thoughts or Judgments			
	Watched and Named Emotions			
	Didn't Act on Emotions			
	Used Opposite Action			
	Used Problem Solving			
Interpersonal Effectiveness	Practiced Compassion for Others			
	Made an Assertive Request			
	Said No Assertively			
	Negotiated Agreements			
	Listened to and Understood Others			
	Validated Others			
Exposure-Based Cognitive Rehearsal	Practiced Exposure-Based Cognitive Rehearsal Skill			
Rate Your Overall Mood for the Day (0 to 10)				

Th	F	Sa	S	NOTES

Core Skills	Coping Strategies	M	T	W
Distress Tolerance	Stopped Self-Destructive Action			
	Used the REST Strategy			
	Used Radical Acceptance			
	Distracted from Pain			
	Engaged in Pleasurable Activities			
	Soothed Myself			
	Practiced Relaxation			
	Committed to Valued Action			
	Rehearsed Values-Based Behavior			
	Connected with My Higher Power			
	Used Coping Thoughts			
	Determined Feelings-Threat Balance			
	Used Coping Strategies			
	Used Physiological-Coping Skills			
Mindfulness	Practiced Mindful Breathing			
	Used Wise Mind			
	Practiced Beginner's Mind			
	Practiced Self-Compassion			
	Used Mindful communication with Others			
	Did What was Effective			
	Completed a Task Mindfully			
Emotion Regulation	Engaged in Physical Regulation of Mood			
	Balanced Thoughts and Feelings			
	Experienced Positive Events			
	Let Go of Thoughts or Judgments			
	Watched and Named Emotions			
	Didn't Act on Emotions			
	Used Opposite Action			
	Used Problem Solving			
Interpersonal Effectiveness	Practiced Compassion for Others			
	Made an Assertive Request			
	Said No Assertively			
	Negotiated Agreements			
	Listened to and Understood Others			
	Validated Others			
Exposure-Based Cognitive Rehearsal	Practiced Exposure-Based Cognitive Rehearsal Skill			
Rate Your Overall Mood for the Day (0 to 10)				

151

Th	F	Sa	S	NOTES

WEEK 44.

Core Skills	Coping Strategies	M	T	W
Distress Tolerance	Stopped Self-Destructive Action			
	Used the REST Strategy			
	Used Radical Acceptance			
	Distracted from Pain			
	Engaged in Pleasurable Activities			
	Soothed Myself			
	Practiced Relaxation			
	Committed to Valued Action			
	Rehearsed Values-Based Behavior			
	Connected with My Higher Power			
	Used Coping Thoughts			
	Determined Feelings-Threat Balance			
	Used Coping Strategies			
	Used Physiological-Coping Skills			
Mindfulness	Practiced Mindful Breathing			
	Used Wise Mind			
	Practiced Beginner's Mind			
	Practiced Self-Compassion			
	Used Mindful communication with Others			
	Did What was Effective			
	Completed a Task Mindfully			
Emotion Regulation	Engaged in Physical Regulation of Mood			
	Balanced Thoughts and Feelings			
	Experienced Positive Events			
	Let Go of Thoughts or Judgments			
	Watched and Named Emotions			
	Didn't Act on Emotions			
	Used Opposite Action			
	Used Problem Solving			
Interpersonal Effectiveness	Practiced Compassion for Others			
	Made an Assertive Request			
	Said No Assertively			
	Negotiated Agreements			
	Listened to and Understood Others			
	Validated Others			
Exposure-Based Cognitive Rehearsal	Practiced Exposure-Based Cognitive Rehearsal Skill			
Rate Your Overall Mood for the Day (0 to 10)				

153

Th	F	Sa	S	NOTES

Core Skills	Coping Strategies	M	T	W
Distress Tolerance	Stopped Self-Destructive Action			
	Used the REST Strategy			
	Used Radical Acceptance			
	Distracted from Pain			
	Engaged in Pleasurable Activities			
	Soothed Myself			
	Practiced Relaxation			
	Committed to Valued Action			
	Rehearsed Values-Based Behavior			
	Connected with My Higher Power			
	Used Coping Thoughts			
	Determined Feelings-Threat Balance			
	Used Coping Strategies			
	Used Physiological-Coping Skills			
Mindfulness	Practiced Mindful Breathing			
	Used Wise Mind			
	Practiced Beginner's Mind			
	Practiced Self-Compassion			
	Used Mindful communication with Others			
	Did What was Effective			
	Completed a Task Mindfully			
Emotion Regulation	Engaged in Physical Regulation of Mood			
	Balanced Thoughts and Feelings			
	Experienced Positive Events			
	Let Go of Thoughts or Judgments			
	Watched and Named Emotions			
	Didn't Act on Emotions			
	Used Opposite Action			
	Used Problem Solving			
Interpersonal Effectiveness	Practiced Compassion for Others			
	Made an Assertive Request			
	Said No Assertively			
	Negotiated Agreements			
	Listened to and Understood Others			
	Validated Others			
Exposure-Based Cognitive Rehearsal	Practiced Exposure-Based Cognitive Rehearsal Skill			
Rate Your Overall Mood for the Day (0 to 10)				

155

Th	F	Sa	S	NOTES

WEEK 46.

Core Skills	Coping Strategies	M	T	W
Distress Tolerance	Stopped Self-Destructive Action			
	Used the REST Strategy			
	Used Radical Acceptance			
	Distracted from Pain			
	Engaged in Pleasurable Activities			
	Soothed Myself			
	Practiced Relaxation			
	Committed to Valued Action			
	Rehearsed Values-Based Behavior			
	Connected with My Higher Power			
	Used Coping Thoughts			
	Determined Feelings-Threat Balance			
	Used Coping Strategies			
	Used Physiological-Coping Skills			
Mindfulness	Practiced Mindful Breathing			
	Used Wise Mind			
	Practiced Beginner's Mind			
	Practiced Self-Compassion			
	Used Mindful communication with Others			
	Did What was Effective			
	Completed a Task Mindfully			
Emotion Regulation	Engaged in Physical Regulation of Mood			
	Balanced Thoughts and Feelings			
	Experienced Positive Events			
	Let Go of Thoughts or Judgments			
	Watched and Named Emotions			
	Didn't Act on Emotions			
	Used Opposite Action			
	Used Problem Solving			
Interpersonal Effectiveness	Practiced Compassion for Others			
	Made an Assertive Request			
	Said No Assertively			
	Negotiated Agreements			
	Listened to and Understood Others			
	Validated Others			
Exposure-Based Cognitive Rehearsal	Practiced Exposure-Based Cognitive Rehearsal Skill			
Rate Your Overall Mood for the Day (0 to 10)				

157

Th	F	Sa	S	NOTES

WEEK 47.

Core Skills	Coping Strategies	M	T	W
Distress Tolerance	Stopped Self-Destructive Action			
	Used the REST Strategy			
	Used Radical Acceptance			
	Distracted from Pain			
	Engaged in Pleasurable Activities			
	Soothed Myself			
	Practiced Relaxation			
	Committed to Valued Action			
	Rehearsed Values-Based Behavior			
	Connected with My Higher Power			
	Used Coping Thoughts			
	Determined Feelings-Threat Balance			
	Used Coping Strategies			
	Used Physiological-Coping Skills			
Mindfulness	Practiced Mindful Breathing			
	Used Wise Mind			
	Practiced Beginner's Mind			
	Practiced Self-Compassion			
	Used Mindful communication with Others			
	Did What was Effective			
	Completed a Task Mindfully			
Emotion Regulation	Engaged in Physical Regulation of Mood			
	Balanced Thoughts and Feelings			
	Experienced Positive Events			
	Let Go of Thoughts or Judgments			
	Watched and Named Emotions			
	Didn't Act on Emotions			
	Used Opposite Action			
	Used Problem Solving			
Interpersonal Effectiveness	Practiced Compassion for Others			
	Made an Assertive Request			
	Said No Assertively			
	Negotiated Agreements			
	Listened to and Understood Others			
	Validated Others			
Exposure-Based Cognitive Rehearsal	Practiced Exposure-Based Cognitive Rehearsal Skill			
Rate Your Overall Mood for the Day (0 to 10)				

159

Th	F	Sa	S	NOTES

WEEK 48.

Core Skills	Coping Strategies	M	T	W
Distress Tolerance	Stopped Self-Destructive Action			
	Used the REST Strategy			
	Used Radical Acceptance			
	Distracted from Pain			
	Engaged in Pleasurable Activities			
	Soothed Myself			
	Practiced Relaxation			
	Committed to Valued Action			
	Rehearsed Values-Based Behavior			
	Connected with My Higher Power			
	Used Coping Thoughts			
	Determined Feelings-Threat Balance			
	Used Coping Strategies			
	Used Physiological-Coping Skills			
Mindfulness	Practiced Mindful Breathing			
	Used Wise Mind			
	Practiced Beginner's Mind			
	Practiced Self-Compassion			
	Used Mindful communication with Others			
	Did What was Effective			
	Completed a Task Mindfully			
Emotion Regulation	Engaged in Physical Regulation of Mood			
	Balanced Thoughts and Feelings			
	Experienced Positive Events			
	Let Go of Thoughts or Judgments			
	Watched and Named Emotions			
	Didn't Act on Emotions			
	Used Opposite Action			
	Used Problem Solving			
Interpersonal Effectiveness	Practiced Compassion for Others			
	Made an Assertive Request			
	Said No Assertively			
	Negotiated Agreements			
	Listened to and Understood Others			
	Validated Others			
Exposure-Based Cognitive Rehearsal	Practiced Exposure-Based Cognitive Rehearsal Skill			
Rate Your Overall Mood for the Day (0 to 10)				

Th	F	Sa	S	NOTES

Core Skills	Coping Strategies	M	T	W
Distress Tolerance	Stopped Self-Destructive Action			
	Used the REST Strategy			
	Used Radical Acceptance			
	Distracted from Pain			
	Engaged in Pleasurable Activities			
	Soothed Myself			
	Practiced Relaxation			
	Committed to Valued Action			
	Rehearsed Values-Based Behavior			
	Connected with My Higher Power			
	Used Coping Thoughts			
	Determined Feelings-Threat Balance			
	Used Coping Strategies			
	Used Physiological-Coping Skills			
Mindfulness	Practiced Mindful Breathing			
	Used Wise Mind			
	Practiced Beginner's Mind			
	Practiced Self-Compassion			
	Used Mindful communication with Others			
	Did What was Effective			
	Completed a Task Mindfully			
Emotion Regulation	Engaged in Physical Regulation of Mood			
	Balanced Thoughts and Feelings			
	Experienced Positive Events			
	Let Go of Thoughts or Judgments			
	Watched and Named Emotions			
	Didn't Act on Emotions			
	Used Opposite Action			
	Used Problem Solving			
Interpersonal Effectiveness	Practiced Compassion for Others			
	Made an Assertive Request			
	Said No Assertively			
	Negotiated Agreements			
	Listened to and Understood Others			
	Validated Others			
Exposure-Based Cognitive Rehearsal	Practiced Exposure-Based Cognitive Rehearsal Skill			
Rate Your Overall Mood for the Day (0 to 10)				

Th	F	Sa	S	NOTES

WEEK 50.

Core Skills	Coping Strategies	M	T	W
Distress Tolerance	Stopped Self-Destructive Action			
	Used the REST Strategy			
	Used Radical Acceptance			
	Distracted from Pain			
	Engaged in Pleasurable Activities			
	Soothed Myself			
	Practiced Relaxation			
	Committed to Valued Action			
	Rehearsed Values-Based Behavior			
	Connected with My Higher Power			
	Used Coping Thoughts			
	Determined Feelings-Threat Balance			
	Used Coping Strategies			
	Used Physiological-Coping Skills			
Mindfulness	Practiced Mindful Breathing			
	Used Wise Mind			
	Practiced Beginner's Mind			
	Practiced Self-Compassion			
	Used Mindful communication with Others			
	Did What was Effective			
	Completed a Task Mindfully			
Emotion Regulation	Engaged in Physical Regulation of Mood			
	Balanced Thoughts and Feelings			
	Experienced Positive Events			
	Let Go of Thoughts or Judgments			
	Watched and Named Emotions			
	Didn't Act on Emotions			
	Used Opposite Action			
	Used Problem Solving			
Interpersonal Effectiveness	Practiced Compassion for Others			
	Made an Assertive Request			
	Said No Assertively			
	Negotiated Agreements			
	Listened to and Understood Others			
	Validated Others			
Exposure-Based Cognitive Rehearsal	Practiced Exposure-Based Cognitive Rehearsal Skill			
Rate Your Overall Mood for the Day (0 to 10)				

Th	F	Sa	S	NOTES

WEEK 51.

Core Skills	Coping Strategies	M	T	W
Distress Tolerance	Stopped Self-Destructive Action			
	Used the REST Strategy			
	Used Radical Acceptance			
	Distracted from Pain			
	Engaged in Pleasurable Activities			
	Soothed Myself			
	Practiced Relaxation			
	Committed to Valued Action			
	Rehearsed Values-Based Behavior			
	Connected with My Higher Power			
	Used Coping Thoughts			
	Determined Feelings-Threat Balance			
	Used Coping Strategies			
	Used Physiological-Coping Skills			
Mindfulness	Practiced Mindful Breathing			
	Used Wise Mind			
	Practiced Beginner's Mind			
	Practiced Self-Compassion			
	Used Mindful communication with Others			
	Did What was Effective			
	Completed a Task Mindfully			
Emotion Regulation	Engaged in Physical Regulation of Mood			
	Balanced Thoughts and Feelings			
	Experienced Positive Events			
	Let Go of Thoughts or Judgments			
	Watched and Named Emotions			
	Didn't Act on Emotions			
	Used Opposite Action			
	Used Problem Solving			
Interpersonal Effectiveness	Practiced Compassion for Others			
	Made an Assertive Request			
	Said No Assertively			
	Negotiated Agreements			
	Listened to and Understood Others			
	Validated Others			
Exposure-Based Cognitive Rehearsal	Practiced Exposure-Based Cognitive Rehearsal Skill			
Rate Your Overall Mood for the Day (0 to 10)				

Th	F	Sa	S	NOTES

WEEK 52.

Core Skills	Coping Strategies	M	T	W
Distress Tolerance	Stopped Self-Destructive Action			
	Used the REST Strategy			
	Used Radical Acceptance			
	Distracted from Pain			
	Engaged in Pleasurable Activities			
	Soothed Myself			
	Practiced Relaxation			
	Committed to Valued Action			
	Rehearsed Values-Based Behavior			
	Connected with My Higher Power			
	Used Coping Thoughts			
	Determined Feelings-Threat Balance			
	Used Coping Strategies			
	Used Physiological-Coping Skills			
Mindfulness	Practiced Mindful Breathing			
	Used Wise Mind			
	Practiced Beginner's Mind			
	Practiced Self-Compassion			
	Used Mindful communication with Others			
	Did What was Effective			
	Completed a Task Mindfully			
Emotion Regulation	Engaged in Physical Regulation of Mood			
	Balanced Thoughts and Feelings			
	Experienced Positive Events			
	Let Go of Thoughts or Judgments			
	Watched and Named Emotions			
	Didn't Act on Emotions			
	Used Opposite Action			
	Used Problem Solving			
Interpersonal Effectiveness	Practiced Compassion for Others			
	Made an Assertive Request			
	Said No Assertively			
	Negotiated Agreements			
	Listened to and Understood Others			
	Validated Others			
Exposure-Based Cognitive Rehearsal	Practiced Exposure-Based Cognitive Rehearsal Skill			
Rate Your Overall Mood for the Day (0 to 10)				

Th	F	Sa	S	NOTES

References

Barrowcliff, A. L., Gray, N. S., MacCulloch, S., Freeman, T. C. A., & MacCulloch, M. J. (2003). Horizontal rhythmical eye movements consistently diminish the arousal provoked by auditory stimuli. *British Journal of Clinical Psychology, 42,* 289–302.

Barrowcliff, A. L., Gray, N. S., Freeman, T. C. A., & MacCulloch, M. J. (2004). Eye movements reduce the vividness, emotional valence, and electrodermal arousal associated with negative autobiographical memories. *Journal of Forensic Psychiatry and Psychology, 15,* 325–345.

Beck, A. T., Rush, A. J., Shaw, B. F., & Emery, G. (1979). *Cognitive therapy of depression.* New York: Guilford Press.

Bower, G. H. (1981). Mood and memory. *American Psychologist, 36*(2), 129-148.

Cautela, J. (1971, September). *Covert Modeling.* Paper presented at the fifth annual meeting of the Association for Advancement of Behavior Therapy, Washington, DC.

Clark, M. E., & Hirschman, R. (1990). Effects of paced respiration on anxiety reduction in a clinical population. *Biofeedback and Self-Regulation, 15*(3), 273–284.

Davis, M., Eshelman, E. R., & McKay, M. (1980). *The relaxation & stress reduction workbook.* Oakland, CA: New Harbinger Publications.

Dishman, R. K. (1997). Brain monoamines, exercise, and behavioral stress: Animal models. *Medicine and Science in Sports and Exercise, 29*(1), 63–74.

Downing, S. (2016). Low, moderate, and high intensity exercise: How to tell the difference. https://coach.nine.com.au/2017/02/01/07/25/exercise-intensity.

Gibala, M. J., & McGee, S. L. (2008). Metabolic adaptations to short-term high-intensity interval training: A little pain for a lot of gain? *Exercise and Sport Sciences Review* 36(2), 58–63.

Gibala, M. J., Little, J. P., MacDonald, M. J., & Hawley, J. A. (2012). Physiological adaptations to low-volume, high-intensity interval training in health and disease. *Journal of Physiology, 590*(Pt. 5), 1077–1084.

Gooden, B. A. (1994). Mechanism of the human diving response. *Integrative Physiological and Behavioral Science, 29*(1), 6–16.

Jacobson, E. (1938). *Progressive relaxation.* (Rev. 2nd ed.) Chicago: University of Chicago Press.

Jung, M. E., Bourne, J. E., & Little, J. P. (2014). Where does HIT fit? An examination of the affective response to high-intensity intervals in comparison to continuous moderate- and continuous vigorous-intensity exercise in the exercise intensity-affect continuum. *PLOS ONE* 9(12): e114541.https://doi.org/10.1371/journal.pone.0114541.

Kinoshita, T., Nagata, S., Baba, R., Kohmoto, T., & Iwagaki, S. (2006). Cold-water face immersion per se elicits cardiac parasympathetic activity. *Circulation Journal, 70*(6), 773–776.

Lehrer, P. M. & Gevirtz, R. (2014, July 21). Heart rate variability biofeedback: How and why does it work? *Frontiers in Psychology,* 5(Article 756): https://www.ncbi.nlm.nih.gov/pmc/articles/PMC4104929/

Linehan, M. M. 1(993a). *Cognitive-behavioral treatment of borderline personality disorder.* New York: Guilford Press.

Linehan, M. M. (1993b). *Skills training manual for treating borderline personality disorder.* New York: Guilford Press.

Linehan, M. M. (2015). *DBT skills training manual, second edition.* New York: Guilford Press.

McCaul, K. D., Solomon, S., & Holmes, D. S. (1979). Effects of paced respiration and expectations on physiological and psychological responses to threat. *Journal of Personality and Social Psychology, 37*(4), 564–571.

McKay, M., Wood, J. C., and Brantley, J. (2007). *The dialectical behavior therapy skills workbook: Practical DBT exercises for learning mindfulness, interpersonal effectiveness, emotion regulation, and distress tolerance.* Oakland, CA: New Harbinger Publications.

McKay, M., & West, A. (2016). *Emotion efficacy therapy: A brief, exposure-based treatment for emotion regulation integrating ACT and DBT.* Oakland, CA: Context Press.

McKay, M., & Wood, J. (2019). *The new happiness: Practices for spiritual growth and living with intention.* Oakland, CA: Reveal Press.

McKay, M., Wood, J., & Brantley, J. (2019). *The dialectical behavior therapy skills workbook, second edition: Practical DBT exercises for learning mindfulness, interpersonal effectiveness, emotion regulation, and distress tolerance.* Oakland, CA: New Harbinger.

Nutt, R.M. & Lam, D. (2011). Comparison of mood-dependent memory in bipolar disorder and normal controls. *Clinical Psychology and Psychotherapy, 18,* 379–386.

Russ, M. J., Roth, S. D., Lerman, A., Kakuma, T., Harrison, K., Shindledecker, R. D., et al. (1992). Pain perception in self-injurious patients with borderline personality disorder. *Biological Psychiatry, 32,* 501–511.

Ströhle, A. (2009). Physical activity, exercise, depression, and anxiety disorders. *Journal of Neural Transmission, 116,* 777–784.

Suzuki, S. (2001). *Zen mind, beginner's mind: Informal talks on zen meditation and practice.* New York: Weatherhill.

Szymanski, J., & O'Donohue, W. (1995). The potential role of state-dependent learning in cognitive therapy with spider phobia. *Journal of Rational-Emotive & Cognitive-Behavior Therapy, 13* (2), 131-150.

Trost, S. G., Owen, N., Bauman, A. E., Sallis, J. F., & Brown, W. (2002). Correlates of adults' participation in physical activity: Review and update. *Medicine & Science in Sports & Exercise, 34,* 1996–2001.

Weingartner, H., Miller, H., & Murphy, D. L. (1977). Mood-state-dependent retrieval of verbal associations. *Journal of Abnormal Psychology, 86*(3), 276-284.

Wolpe, J. (1958). *Psychotherapy by reciprocal inhibition.* Stanford, CA: Stanford University Press.

Matthew McKay, PhD, is a professor at the Wright Institute in Berkeley, CA. He has authored and coauthored numerous books, including *The Dialectical Behavior Therapy Skills Workbook*, *The Relaxation and Stress Reduction Workbook*, *Self-Esteem*, *Thoughts and Feelings*, *When Anger Hurts*, and *ACT on Life Not on Anger*. McKay received his PhD in clinical psychology from the California School of Professional Psychology, and specializes in the cognitive behavioral treatment of anxiety and depression.

Jeffrey C. Wood, PsyD, lives and works in Las Vegas, NV. He specializes in brief therapy treatments for depression, anxiety, and trauma. He also provides coaching for spiritual development, communication skills development, and life skills. Wood is coauthor of *The New Happiness*, *The Dialectical Behavior Therapy Skills Workbook*, and *The Dialectical Behavior Therapy Diary*.

ABOUT NEW HARBINGER

Founded by psychologist Matthew McKay and Patrick Fanning, New Harbinger has published books that promote wellness in mind, body, and spirit for more than forty-five years.

Our proven-effective self-help books and pioneering workbooks help readers of all ages and backgrounds make positive lifestyle changes, improve mental health and well-being, and achieve meaningful personal growth. In addition, our spirituality books offer profound guidance for deepening awareness and cultivating healing, self-discovery, and fulfillment.

New Harbinger is proud to be an independent and employee-owned company, publishing books that reflect its core values of integrity, innovation, commitment, sustainability, compassion, and trust. Written by leaders in the field and recommended by therapists worldwide, New Harbinger books are practical, reliable, and provide real tools for real change.

 **newharbinger**publications

MORE BOOKS from
NEW HARBINGER PUBLICATIONS

**THE DIALECTICAL
BEHAVIOR THERAPY
SKILLS CARD DECK**

52 Practices to Balance Your
Emotions Every Day

978-1684033980 / US $16.95

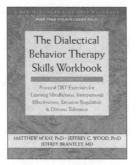

**THE DIALECTICAL
BEHAVIOR THERAPY
SKILLS WORKBOOK,
SECOND EDITION**

Practical DBT Exercises for Learning
Mindfulness, Interpersonal
Effectiveness, Emotion Regulation,
and Distress Tolerance

978-1684034581 / US $24.95

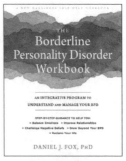

**THE BORDERLINE
PERSONALITY DISORDER
WORKBOOK**

An Integrative Program to
Understand and Manage
Your BPD

978-1684032730 / US $24.95

**BOUNCING BACK
FROM REJECTION**

Build the Resilience You
Need to Get Back Up When
Life Knocks You Down

978-1684034024 / US $16.95

**ADULT CHILDREN
OF EMOTIONALLY
IMMATURE PARENTS**

How to Heal from Distant,
Rejecting, or Self-Involved Parents

978-1626251700 / US $18.95

**THOUGHTS AND
FEELINGS,
FIFTH EDITION**

Taking Control of Your Moods
and Your Life

978-1684035489 / US $25.95

🌺 **newharbinger**publications

1-800-748-6273 / newharbinger.com

(VISA, MC, AMEX / prices subject to change without notice)

Follow Us 🟦📘🐦▶️📌in